Harnessing Water Power

Living Things of Today

Weather Instruments

The Golden Book of
SCIENCE

REVISED EDITION

THE GOLDEN BOOK OF
SCIENCE

by Bertha Morris Parker

FORMERLY OF THE LABORATORY SCHOOLS, UNIVERSITY OF CHICAGO

RESEARCH ASSOCIATE, CHICAGO NATURAL HISTORY MUSEUM

ILLUSTRATED by Harry McNaught

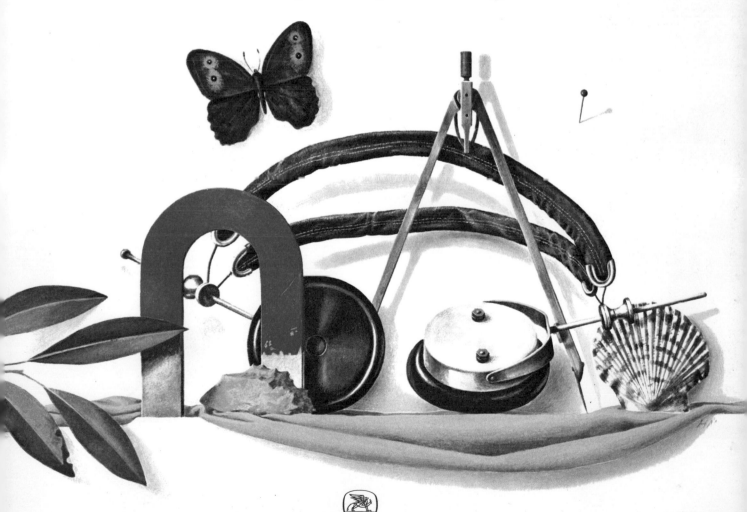

GOLDEN PRESS · NEW YORK

CONTENTS

Revised Edition—Second Printing, 1964

LIBRARY OF CONGRESS CATALOG CARD NUMBER: 63-14917

© COPYRIGHT 1963, 1956 BY GOLDEN PRESS, INC. DESIGNED AND PRODUCED BY ARTISTS AND WRITERS PRESS, INC. ALL RIGHTS RESERVED, INCLUDING THE RIGHT OF REPRODUCTION IN WHOLE OR IN PART IN ANY FORM. PRINTED IN THE U.S.A. BY WESTERN PRINTING AND LITHOGRAPHING CO. PUBLISHED BY GOLDEN PRESS, INC., NEW YORK. PUBLISHED SIMULTANEOUSLY IN CANADA BY THE MUSSON BOOK CO., LTD., TORONTO

HOW OLD IS OLD?

GRASSHOPPERS live only a few months. They hatch out in the spring and die before cold weather. A grasshopper six months old is an old grasshopper.

A dog six months old is still a puppy. A dog is not old until it is at least 12 years old. A 12-year-old dog is about as old for a dog as a 70-year-old man is for a man.

Not many animals live to be older than the oldest people. It is a common idea that elephants live for a very long time. But a 60-year-old elephant can be called really old. Some big tortoises *are* longer-lived than people. A giant tortoise is not old until it is more than 100.

Sunflowers live for only one summer. So do many other plants. But some plants live to be much, much older. The oldest plants we know about are trees. The oldest trees are far, far older than the oldest animals. Some of the big trees of California are three or four thousand years old!

But the oldest big tree is young compared with the Rocky Mountains. They are millions of years old. Scientists, however, call the Rocky Mountains young. They are millions of years younger than the mountains in the eastern part of our country.

Of course, the earth had to be here before there could be any mountains or any living things on it. Scientists cannot tell surely how long there has been an earth. Probably the earth is at least four billion years old!

Whale and Elephant

HOW BIG IS BIG?

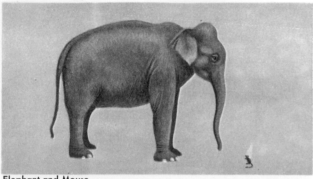
Elephant and Mouse

Flea and Millions of Bacteria

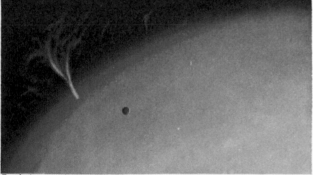
Earth Against the Sun

"As BIG as an elephant" we say when we want to tell that something is very big. But an elephant is not very big compared with a blue whale. It would take at least 20 elephants to weigh as much as one blue whale.

Although an elephant is not nearly so big as a whale, it is certainly a giant beside a mouse.

We think of a mouse as a little animal. But a mouse is many times as big as a flea.

The tiny plants we call bacteria are so tiny that they cannot be seen at all without a microscope. They are so small that millions and millions of them would be needed to take up as much space as one flea takes up.

But even bacteria are big compared with atoms. Atoms are the tiny, tiny, tiny particles everything in the world is made up of. The tiniest atoms are far too small to be seen with any microscope.

A whale is enormous. But it is not very big compared with a mountain. No one mountain is very big compared with the earth. And the earth is by no means the biggest thing we know about. The sun is so much bigger that, if it were hollow, there would be room for a million earths inside it.

But even the sun is not the last word in bigness. There are stars that are millions of times as big as our sun. And even the biggest star is only a tiny part of the whole universe. "From atom to universe" is one way of saying "from little to big."

Portion of the Universe Seen Through a Telescope

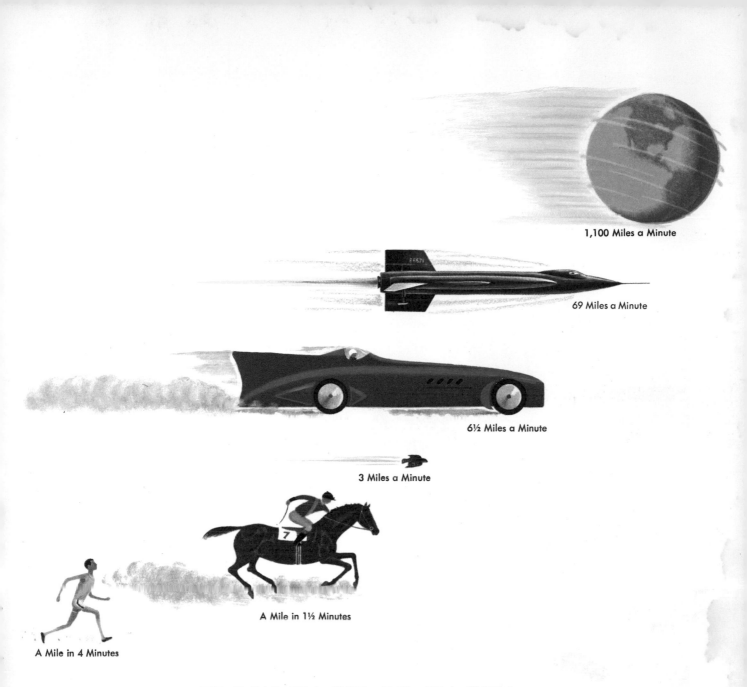

1,100 Miles a Minute

69 Miles a Minute

6½ Miles a Minute

3 Miles a Minute

A Mile in 1½ Minutes

A Mile in 4 Minutes

HOW FAST IS FAST?

THE FASTEST human runners can run a mile in a little less than four minutes. Race horses are faster. The fastest can run a mile in a little more than a minute and a half. The fastest birds, however, could win any race with a race horse. The peregrine falcon has been timed at three miles a minute.

Automobiles are faster still. The fastest racing automobiles can go six and a half miles in a minute. But even a racing car is slow beside a fast plane. For a long time the builders of planes tried to make a plane that would travel as fast as sound. Sound travels about 12 miles a minute. At last plane builders succeeded in making jet planes that could win a race with sound. Rocket planes launched high in the air go still faster. The record is more than 4,000 miles an hour.

But even the fastest rocket plane is a slowpoke compared with the earth. The earth travels in a big, big circle around the sun every year. To get all the way around in a year it has to travel 18½ miles every second! This means that it travels about 1,100 miles a minute!

Can anything be faster? Yes! Light, for instance, is much faster. It travels 186,000 miles in a single second! We do not know of anything that travels faster than that.

9

HOW FAR IS FAR?

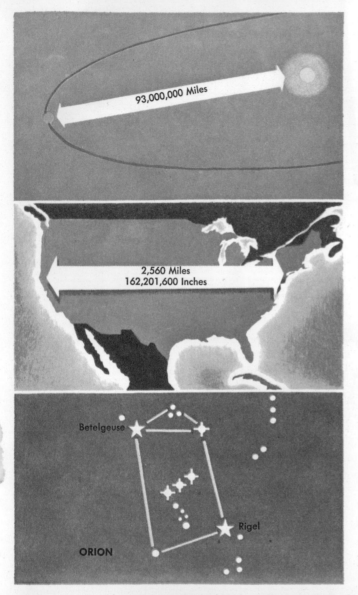

93,000,000 Miles

2,560 Miles
162,201,600 Inches

Betelgeuse

Rigel

ORION

A BOY who lives a mile from school thinks he has a long way to go every morning. But a mile is only a step when we think of the distance around the earth. The earth at the equator is nearly 25,000 miles around. But even a trip around the earth would be short compared with a trip to the sun. The sun is about 93,000,000 miles away.

It is hard to think of anything farther away than that. But the sun is a close neighbor compared with the stars. The stars are so far away that just telling how far away they are in miles does not mean much. It is like telling how many inches it is from New York to San Francisco. Scientists tell us how far away stars are by telling us how long it takes light to get to us from them. Light, traveling 186,000 miles a second, still needs nearly nine years to reach us from the Dog Star, the brightest star in the sky.

Even the Dog Star is a near neighbor compared with Rigel, the brightest star in the group of stars called Orion. The light that reaches our eyes when we look up at Rigel started on its way to us 500 years before Columbus discovered America!

But even Rigel is a near neighbor compared with the big swirl of stars the picture below shows. This great swirl looks like a little fuzzy star when we see it without a telescope. It is so far away that its light takes more than two million years to reach us. And there are millions and millions and millions of stars that are farther away than that!

Great Nebula in Andromeda

HOW HOT IS HOT?

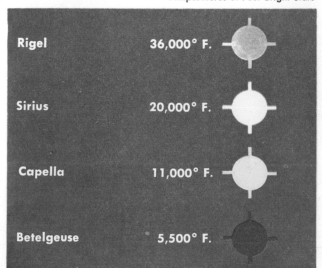

Sun

A DAY when the thermometer says 100 degrees is a very hot day. People have to be careful not to get a sunstroke on a day as hot as that. Of course, there may be even hotter days. The thermometer has gone up to 134 degrees in Death Valley, California.

Boiling water is much hotter than the air on even the hottest day. The temperature of boiling water is about 212 degrees. How pure the water is and how high it is above the level of the sea make a difference in how hot it is when it is boiling.

In ovens for baking the temperatures go to 500 degrees or even higher. Four hundred and twenty-five degrees is good for baking pie. Furnaces are hotter still. In an electric furnace it is easy to get a temperature of 7,000 degrees.

But the very hottest furnace is not very hot compared with the sun. The temperature of the outside of the sun is about 11,000 degrees. And at the center the temperature is about 20,000,000 degrees! The sun is made partly of iron and silver and lead. But iron and silver and lead are not solid there. The sun is so hot that these metals are gases.

Hot as it is, the sun is not so hot as some of the stars. All stars are suns, but some are much hotter than others. Stars give away the secret of how hot they are by their color. Yellow stars are all about the same temperature as our sun. They are hotter than red stars, but they are not so hot as white stars. And blue stars are the hottest of all. Some are over 50,000 degrees at the surface.

Electric Furnace for Making Steel

Temperatures of Four Bright Stars

Rigel	36,000° F.
Sirius	20,000° F.
Capella	11,000° F.
Betelgeuse	5,500° F.

Golden Garden Spider

Tiger Swallowtail Butterfly

A MILLION KINDS OF ANIMALS

IN THE whole world there are about a million kinds of animals. In size they range all the way from the huge blue whale down to animals much too small to be seen without a microscope.

The bodies of all animals are built of tiny blocks of living material called cells. Our own bodies are made of billions of cells. The bodies of the tiniest animals are made of just one cell. All the one-celled animals are called protozoa. This name means "first animals." The earliest animals must have been one-celled.

Most kinds of animals can move about. Some can fly; some can swim; some can hop; some can run; some can crawl. But some stay in one place all their lives. The simple animals called sponges, for instance, grow fast to rocks and stay there.

More than three-fourths of all the kinds of animals in the world are insects. Birds make up a big group of animals, but there are 90 times as many kinds of insects as of birds. Snails, clams, and their close relatives make up a great group, too, but it is not nearly so big as the insect group.

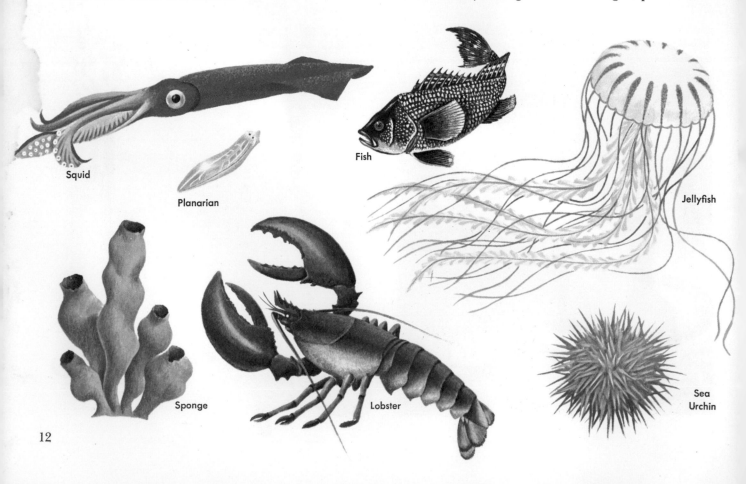

Squid

Planarian

Fish

Jellyfish

Sponge

Lobster

Sea Urchin

Blue Jay

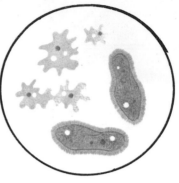

Protozoa Magnified

Down its back every bird has a row of bones that we call a backbone. Four other groups of animals have backbones. They are the fishes, the amphibians, the reptiles, and the mammals. There are about as many kinds of fishes as there are kinds of birds. Almost everyone knows some of them. Almost everyone knows some of the amphibians and some of the reptiles, too. Toads and frogs are amphibians. Snakes and turtles are reptiles. Everyone is very sure to know at least one kind of mammal. For people are mammals. Mammals are animals with hair or fur.

Scientists have a long name for animals with backbones. They call them vertebrates. They have an even longer name for insects, snails, clams, and all the other animals without backbones. Animals without backbones are invertebrates.

Scarlet Snake

Green Frog

Giraffe

Golden-crowned Kinglet

Yellow Warbler

Redstart

Field Sparrow

Scarlet Tanager

Indigo Bunting

Barn Swallow

Meadowlark

ANIMALS WITH FEATHERS

ALL BIRDS have feathers. And every animal with feathers is a bird. Feathers make a good covering. They shed water because they are a little oily. And they are as good as fur for keeping warm.

All birds are alike in many other ways. They are all two-legged. They are all warm-blooded—their bodies are warm even in cold weather. They all have two wings. And they all have bills. It is easy to tell birds from other animals.

There are thousands of kinds of birds. Different birds live in different kinds of places. Some of them are fitted in special ways for living where they do. Many shore birds, for instance, have long legs for wading, and many water birds have webbed feet that help them swim.

Although all birds have wings, they cannot all fly. The ostrich is one of the birds that cannot fly. It runs along the ground. The penguin is another bird whose wings cannot lift it off the ground. But the wings make good paddles for swimming.

The ostrich is the biggest bird of today. There were once bigger birds. There was once, for instance, a bird that had a head as big as the head of a horse. But the ostrich is a giant compared with a tiny hummingbird. A full-grown ostrich may weigh 300 pounds. A hummingbird weighs less than a penny.

Mallard Ducks

Ostrich

Penguin

Great Blue Heron

Baltimore Oriole

Cooper's Hawk

Screech Owl

Red-headed
Woodpecker

Cardinal

Ruby-throated
Hummingbirds

Rose-breasted
Grosbeak

Goldfinch

Red-breasted
Nuthatches

Not all birds eat the same kinds of food. The shape of a bird's bill helps us guess what kind of food the bird eats. Owls and hawks have sharp, curved bills that help them tear apart the mice and other small animals they catch. Cardinals, rose-breasted grosbeaks, and goldfinches have short, thick bills good for cracking weed seeds. Nuthatches have thin, sharp little bills that can pick insects from tiny cracks in bark. Woodpeckers have bills so strong that they can dig into wood to get insects. Hummingbirds have bills long enough to reach down into flowers for nectar.

All birds come from eggs. A bird's bill helps it build a nest for its eggs as well as catch its food. Its bill takes the place of hands. An oriole's nest shows what wonderful hands a bill can be.

ANIMALS WITH HAIR

ALL ANIMALS with hair are mammals. And all mammals have at least some hair. Many have a coat of hair so soft and thick that it is called fur. Others, such as the hippopotamus and the armadillo, have only a few bristles. No animals except mammals have any hair at all. Mammals are also the only animals that feed their babies with milk from their own bodies. They are, moreover, the only animals besides birds that are warm-blooded.

The babies of most mammals are born, not hatched. But there are two mammals that lay eggs. They are the duckbill and the spiny anteater. There are some other mammals whose babies are very, very tiny and helpless when they are born. Their mothers carry them about in pouches on their bodies for weeks or even months. The kangaroo, the opossum, and the koala are pouched mammals. There are others, too. Most of the pouched mammals and both the egg-laying mammals live in Australia.

Most mammals can be called beasts, for they are four-legged. But some are not beasts. Bats are furry. They feed their babies milk. They are clearly mammals. But they fly about. They cannot walk at all. The very biggest mammals—the whales—are not four-legged either. Their ancestors probably lived on land and walked on four legs, but whales have flippers instead of legs. In the seas there are other mammals without legs. The most important mammals of all are two-legged. These most important mammals, of course, are people.

Some mammals eat nothing but meat. Some eat nothing but plants. Others eat both meat and plants, just as we do.

Koala

Duckbill, or Platypus

Armadillo

Spiny Anteater, or Echidna

Squirrel

Giant Anteater

Opossum

Kangaroo

Rabbit

Cow

Pig

Dog

Goat

Tiger

Zebra

Raccoon

Camel

Bear

Hippopotamus

17

FISHES

THE FIRST animals with backbones were fishes. They were a great success. There are still thousands and thousands of kinds of fishes. The fish of our rivers and lakes and seas furnish food for millions of people.

Some fishes live all their lives in fresh water. They live in ponds and lakes and streams. The whitefish and the perch are fresh-water fishes. So are most of the catfishes.

Some fishes live all their lives in salt water. The cod and the herring are salt-water fishes.

Some fishes spend part of their lives in salt water and part in fresh water. The eel and the salmon are two of them.

Fishes are well fitted for living in water. They have fins for swimming. They have gills for breathing. Most of them can move through water easily because they are streamlined. Most of them are protected by scales.

Of course, fishes must find their food in the water about them. Many catch such animals as insects, worms, and smaller fish. Many others live on a "soup" made up of very tiny plants and animals. We call this "soup" plankton.

Catfish

Hammerhead Shark

Yellow Perch

Whitefish

Salmon

Herring

Cod

Eel

Flounder

Sea Horses

Ocean Sunfish

It is easy to tell that most fishes are fishes. But some have queer shapes. The hammerhead shark has its eyes on stalks. The ocean sunfish is almost all head. The tiny sea horse has a thin tail it can twist around seaweed. The flounder is flat and has both its eyes on the same side of its head. The eel is long and rather like a snake.

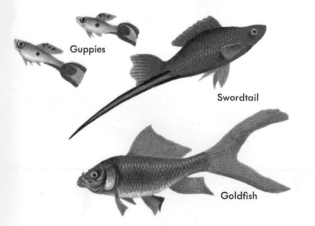

Guppies

Swordtail

Goldfish

In the waters of tropical lands there are many beautiful little fishes. Some of them can be kept in aquariums. The guppy and the swordtail are two that make good aquarium fishes. These little tropical fishes do not lay eggs as most fishes do. The mother fish carry the eggs in their bodies until they grow into tiny fish.

Goldfish are our commonest aquarium fishes. They have been raised for aquariums for hundreds of years.

People used to call any animal that lives in water a fish. "Fish" is still a part of the name of many animals that are not fishes. The starfish is not a true fish. The jellyfish, cuttlefish, and crayfish are not true fishes either. None of these animals has a backbone. Many people still think of whales as fishes. They would soon change their minds if they saw a baby whale nursing.

19

Life History of a Frog

OTHER ANIMALS WITH BACKBONES

SUPPOSE an animal has a backbone. Suppose, too, it is not a bird or a mammal or a fish. Then it must be one of two things. It must be either an amphibian or a reptile.

The first amphibian is sometimes called "the fish that walked." When they are young, most amphibians look much like baby fish. They live in water and breathe with gills. But when they grow up, most of them have legs. They breathe with lungs and live at least part of the time on land.

The name "amphibian" means "living in two places." It is a good name for these animals.

Toads, frogs, newts, and salamanders are amphibians. The mud puppy is also an amphibian (it is a salamander), even though it does not follow the usual amphibian plan of living. It lives in water and breathes with gills all its life.

Many people have watched toads and frogs grow up. It is easy to get toad eggs or frog eggs in the spring and keep them in an aquarium. The eggs hatch into tiny tadpoles. The tadpoles grow. In time hind legs grow out of their bodies. Then front legs grow. The tails disappear. The tiny water animals have become four-legged animals that can breathe air and live on land. They now eat animals instead of plants.

There are fewer kinds of amphibians than there are kinds of birds or mammals or fishes. The group is not very important.

Reptiles start their lives on land. Some of them then go to rivers or ponds or lakes or seas and spend the rest of their lives there. But most reptiles are always land animals. Even those that live part of their lives in water breathe with lungs.

AMPHIBIANS

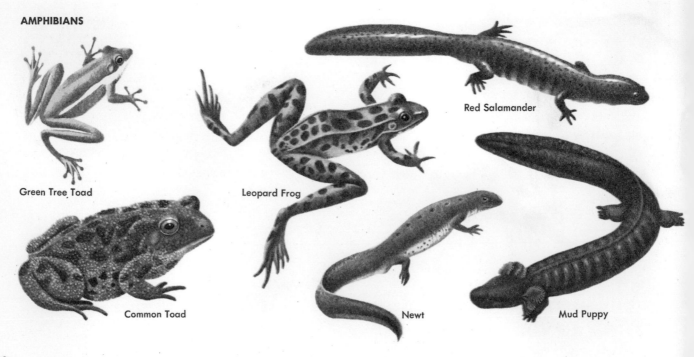

Green Tree Toad

Leopard Frog

Red Salamander

Common Toad

Newt

Mud Puppy

Some reptiles are big; some are little. Some have four legs; some have no legs at all. Some are dangerous; some are our helpers.

At a glance no one would think of an alligator and a garter snake and a painted turtle as being close relatives. But they are all reptiles. All snakes and turtles are reptiles. All alligators and crocodiles are reptiles. All lizards are reptiles, too.

A grown-up salamander and a lizard are about the same shape. But it is really very easy to tell them apart. Salamanders have smooth, bare skin. Lizards are covered with scales. All amphibians have bare skin, although toads have little warty-looking bumps on their skin. Almost all reptiles are covered with scales. The turtles have shells besides.

There are more kinds of reptiles than there are kinds of amphibians. But there were once ever and ever so many more reptiles than there are now. There was a time far back in the earth's history called the Age of Reptiles. That was long before there were people on the earth. In those days there were even big flying reptiles. We are not sorry that they have disappeared.

REPTILES

Flying Reptiles of Long Ago

Garter Snake

Painted Turtles

Fence Lizard

Alligator

Starfish

Egg Cases of Sea Snail

Sand Dollar

SEA SHELLS

ONE of the reasons it is fun to go to the seashore is that there are always shells to gather. Most of the shells are empty when we find them on the shore, but they were all once the homes of animals that lived along the seacoasts. They were once the homes of snails and clams and other animals without backbones.

A snail has only one part to its house. As a rule its single shell is coiled. A clam's shell, on the other hand, has two parts. The two halves open and close. Thousands of kinds of seashore animals follow the clam pattern in building their houses. More thousands follow the snail pattern.

Most seashore animals make their own shells. They make them out of lime from the water. When a teakettle is used for a long time, a layer of lime from the water collects on the inside. This lime is not at all pretty. But it is the same stuff the seashore animals use to build their beautiful shells.

One kind of animal is often found in a shell it did not make for itself. A hermit crab takes over an empty snail shell for its home.

Some shells have names that tell us a great deal about how they look. "Bleeding tooth," "angel wing," "boat shell," "turkey wing," and "auger shell" are a few of them.

The same kind of animal may make shells of many different colors. Butterfly shells, for instance, are wonderful shells to collect because they can be found in many colors. Scallop shells come in many different colors, too.

Living Hard-shell Clam, or Quahog

Living Banded Tulip Snail

Hermit Crab in Moon Shell

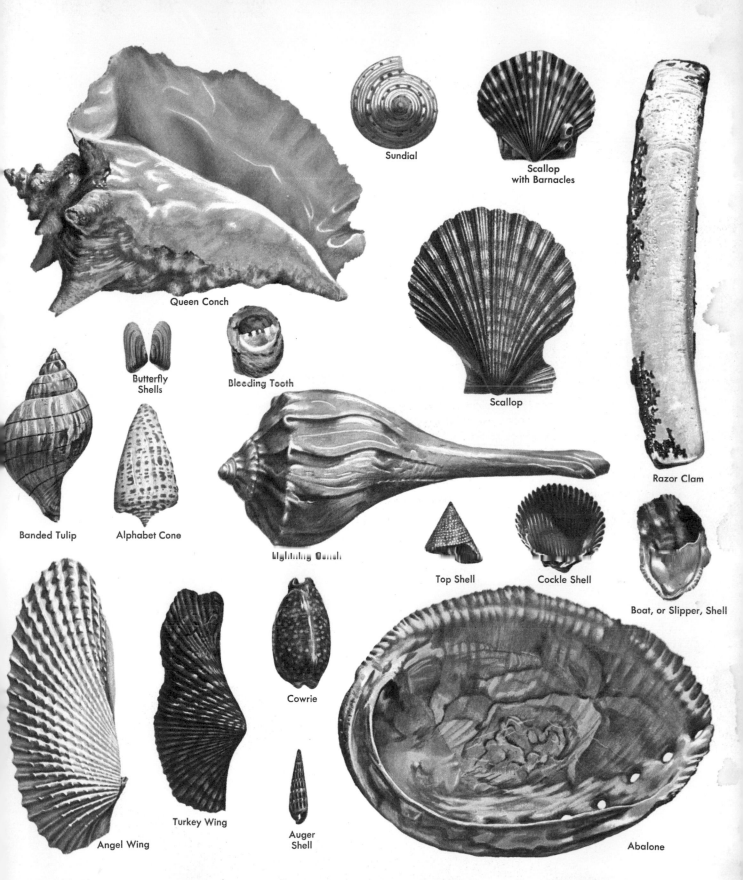

Queen Conch

Sundial

Scallop
with Barnacles

Butterfly
Shells

Bleeding Tooth

Scallop

Banded Tulip

Alphabet Cone

Lightning Conch

Top Shell

Cockle Shell

Razor Clam

Boat, or Slipper, Shell

Angel Wing

Turkey Wing

Cowrie

Auger
Shell

Abalone

There are thousands and thousands of different kinds of sea shells. Some of them measure as much as a foot. Others are tiny specks almost too small to be seen without a microscope. No one has all the kinds of shells there are. A shell collector never runs out of something to do.

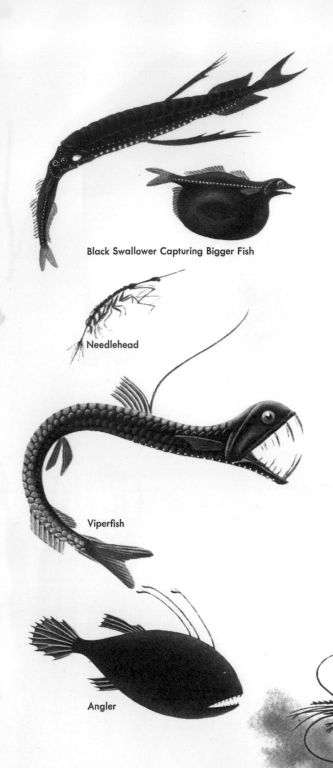

Black Swallower Capturing Bigger Fish

Needlehead

Viperfish

Angler

Shrimp

Bathysphere Fish

IN THE DEEP SEA

VERY FEW people have ever seen any of these animals alive. They are animals of the deep sea.

Deep in the sea where they live it is very dark. Sunlight cannot shine down through the water that far.

Water is heavy. It pushes with great force on anything far down in it. All these animals are able to stand the great pressure of the water. They are so well fitted for standing this pressure that they are not able to live near the surface. When deep-sea fishes are caught in nets and raised to the surface, they are likely to blow up.

All the animals of the deep sea are meat eaters. No green plants can grow in the darkness.

It must be hard for these deep-sea creatures to find food. Some of them give off light of their own that may help. The angler, for instance, has glowing spots that are like little lanterns. They may attract other animals. They may help the angler see its prey.

Many deep-sea fishes have big heads and long, sharp teeth. If one of these creatures catches a smaller animal, the animal does not have much of a chance to get away. These fishes do not all have to live on smaller animals. A black swallower can swallow a fish much bigger than it is.

Not all the deep-sea creatures are fishes. Many are cousins of our lobsters and crabs.

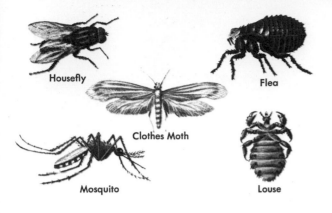

Housefly

Flea

Clothes Moth

Mosquito

Louse

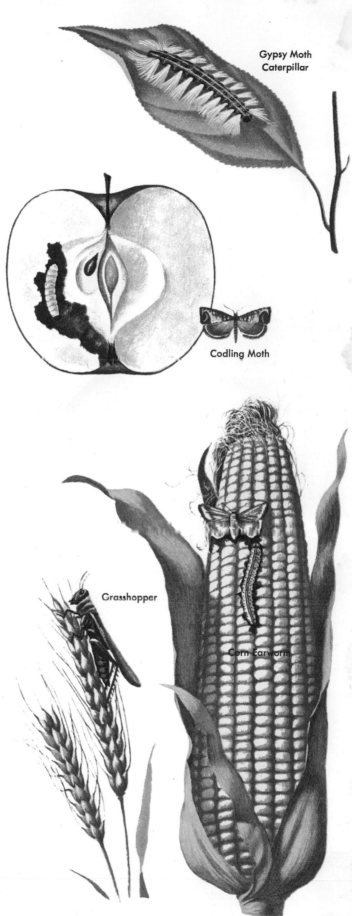

Gypsy Moth Caterpillar

Codling Moth

Grasshopper

Corn Earworm

INSECT ENEMIES

THERE are more than three-quarters of a million kinds of insects. And there are ever and ever so many insects of each kind. No wonder some of them get in our way and are a nuisance.

Insects have to have food. Some of them eat food we want for ourselves. They eat the grain we raise on our farms and the vegetables in our gardens and the fruit in our orchards. Every time we find a wormy apple or potato or ear of corn we can say, "Our six-legged neighbors got there first." For the "worms" in apples and potatoes and ears of corn are not real worms. They are baby insects instead. Many insects are like worms when they are young. Some of these wormlike baby insects we call caterpillars. Some we call grubs. Others we call worms.

Some insects even come to our tables and try to take food off our plates. Houseflies are a big nuisance in this way.

Some insects are our enemies because they hurt our forest and shade trees. They may eat the leaves. They may bore into the trunk or the roots.

Some insects eat holes in our clothes and our carpets. Some harm our books. Some may even eat the wood in the walls of our houses.

But the most harmful insects are the ones that carry diseases. Flies, fleas, lice, and mosquitoes are among the disease carriers. They are real enemies.

Termites

Bumblebee

Praying Mantis

Hive of Honeybees

Ladybug

Carrion Beetle

INSECT FRIENDS

No ONE should get the idea that *all* insects are our enemies. Many of the thousands and thousands of insects do not get in our way at all. And some are our very good friends.

The honeybee has been a friend for a long, long time. Probably even cave men often found a bee tree and ate the honey the bees had stored up.

Even if honeybees did not make honey, they would be our friends. For they carry the flower dust called pollen from flower to flower. Carrying pollen helps make seeds and fruits grow. Hives of bees are a common sight in apple orchards.

Bumblebees are especially good friends of farmers that raise red clover. They carry clover pollen from flower to flower and help make clover seed develop.

Some kinds of insects form clean-up squads. Carrion beetles, for instance, eat up dead animals.

Many of our insect friends are friends because they eat insects that are our enemies. The praying

mantis and the common ladybug are two insects that are always welcome in our gardens. The praying mantis is sometimes called an insect tiger because it is such a killer. In some countries, people make a pet of the praying mantis to keep away insect enemies. The ladybug is not so fierce a killer. But it eats a great many plant lice.

The silkworm moth is another of our good friends. Baby silkworm moths are called silkworms. We get all our true silk from the cocoons silkworms spin for themselves.

Life History of Silkworm Moth

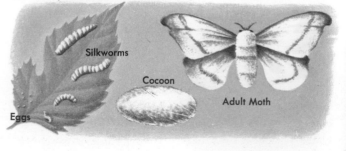

Silkworms

Cocoon

Adult Moth

Eggs

Inside a Hive of Honeybees

INSECT CITIES

INSECTS HAD cities long before people had them. In fact, they had cities long before there were any people on the earth at all. In our cities different people do different kinds of work. They help one another by the work that they do. In an insect city different insects do different kinds of work. By their work they help the whole group.

Not all kinds of insects live in big groups and divide up the work to be done. Some kinds of wasps do. Some kinds of bees do. All kinds of ants do. So do all kinds of termites.

The biggest insect cities are the termite cities. There may be several million termites in one group.

Honeybee cities are much smaller. A big one has about 75,000 bees in it. But no insect cities are more interesting. In a honeybee city, or hive, there is one queen bee. She lays eggs. There are some male bees, or drones. Their only work is to make the eggs of the queen bee fertile so that they will hatch. All the thousands of other bees in the group are worker bees.

There are many different jobs for the worker bees. Some build honeycomb out of wax from their bodies. Some gather pollen and the sweet flower juice called nectar. They fill some of the little "rooms" in the honeycomb with it. Some are living fans. They move their wings very fast to bring fresh air into the hive. Some are nurses. They feed the baby bees. There are still other kinds of work. Guarding the hive, keeping it clean, waiting on the queen bee, and mending cracks in the hive with bee glue are some of them.

The workers all do their work without any quarreling. People can learn a lesson about living together from these insects.

Ducks Migrating

Pony in Winter

Bear Hibernating

SPENDING THE WINTER

MANY ANIMALS cannot stand cold weather. In fact, many kinds of small animals die when winter comes on. They leave only their eggs to live through the time of snow and ice.

In the winter we put on heavy clothes. Some animals grow heavy coats of their own. The pony in the picture has on his shaggy winter coat.

In our houses we can shut the doors and windows and make a fire in the furnace. No other animals can build a fire to keep themselves warm, but some animals do find snug winter homes for themselves. A frog buries itself in mud at the bottom of a pond. A bear curls up in a hollow tree. A chipmunk stays in a home underground. These animals sleep most of the time. Spending the winter in this way is called hibernating.

Instead of trying to keep warm in cold weather, some people travel to places where it is warm. They come back when winter is over. Some animals follow this same plan. They travel to warmer regions for the winter. In the spring they come back to their summer homes.

Traveling in this way is called migrating. The monarch butterfly is one animal that migrates. The caribou is another. But by far the best known of the animals that migrate are birds.

Some birds fly thousands of miles every spring and every fall. How they can find their way on their long journeys is a great mystery.

Bumblebee

Bumblebee Moth

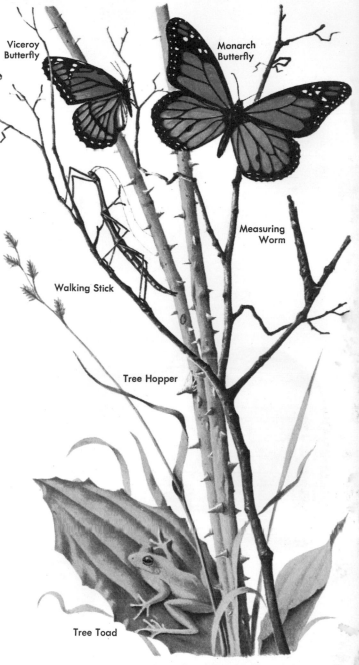

Viceroy Butterfly

Monarch Butterfly

Measuring Worm

Walking Stick

Tree Hopper

Tree Toad

COPYCATS

EVERY ANIMAL has to have food. And most kinds of animals are good food for other animals. How to get something to eat and not be eaten up is a big problem in the animal world. Some animals can escape from their enemies because they are able to fly or swim or run fast. Some have weapons or armor for protecting themselves. Some escape from their enemies by being copycats.

Many animals copy the colors of the things around them. They match their surroundings so well that they are hard to see. Some even change their color if their surroundings change. The little tree toad is pale gray when it is resting on the bark of a birch tree. Some animals copy the shape as well as the color of something in their surroundings. As its name tells, the walking stick looks like a stick, or twig. The measuring worm looks like a twig, too, when it rises up from the branch it is on. It is hard to tell the tiny tree hopper from a thorn. The fringes on its body as well as its pattern of colors make the mousefish match the seaweed around it.

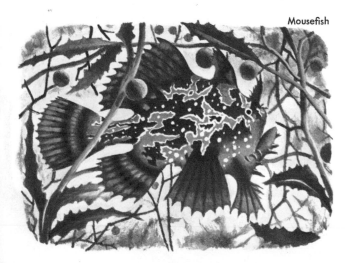

Mousefish

The viceroy butterfly is a famous copycat. Its shape and colors do not help it hide. Instead, they make it look like the monarch butterfly. The monarch butterfly has such a bad taste that birds leave it alone. They leave the viceroy alone, too.

An animal may copy another animal that has a good weapon. The bumblebee moth is harmless. It does not have a stinger. But it looks so much like a bumblebee that its enemies pass it by.

Of course, no one can tell exactly how much it helps all these animals to look like something else. But it is a good guess that many of them would have disappeared if they hadn't been copycats.

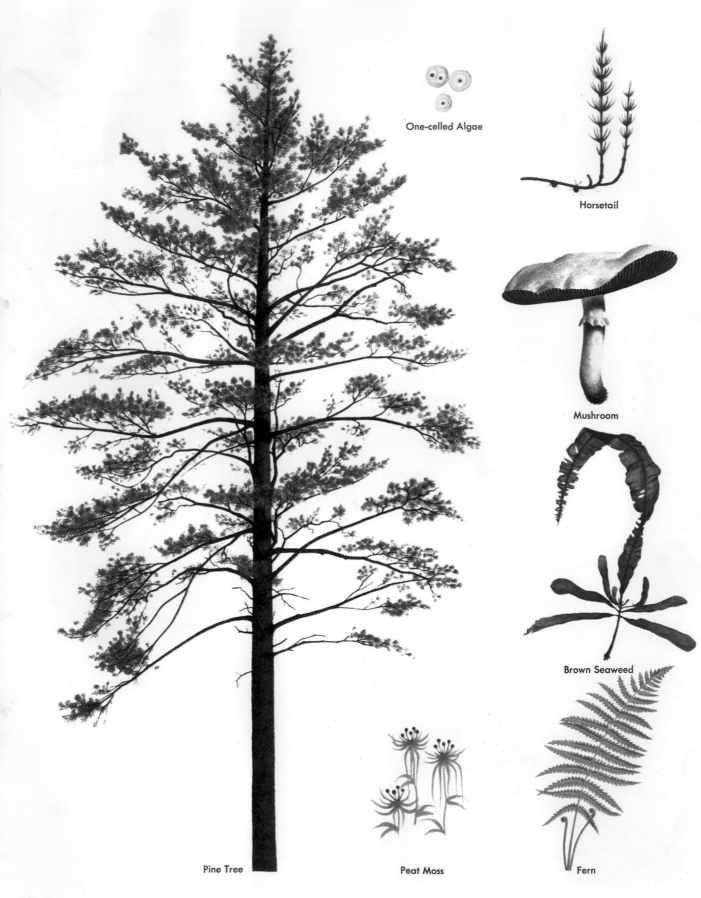

One-celled Algae

Horsetail

Mushroom

Brown Seaweed

Pine Tree

Peat Moss

Fern

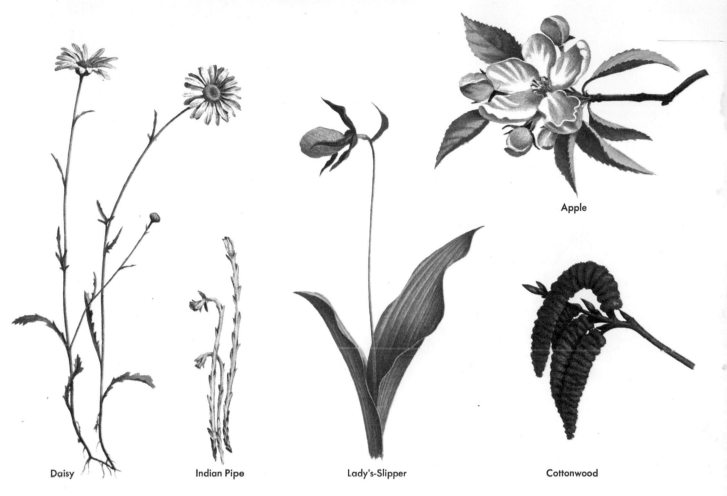

Daisy   Indian Pipe   Lady's-Slipper   Apple   Cottonwood

HUNDREDS OF THOUSANDS OF PLANTS

THERE ARE not so many kinds of plants as there are kinds of animals. But there are a very great many. There are more than 300,000.

In size, plants range all the way from giants 350 feet tall to some so tiny that they are far too small to be seen without a powerful microscope. The smallest plants, like the smallest animals, are one-celled. Big plants, like big animals, are made of millions or billions of cells.

Trees are our biggest plants. Trees are so big that many people are surprised to find out that they are plants. But a tree is really built very much like a sunflower. It has roots that grow down into the ground. It has a stem, or trunk, that grows up into the air. It has leaves that spread out in the sunshine.

Most plants stay in one place all their lives. No one ever saw a rosebush walking about or a sea-weed crawling along the seashore. But some tiny water plants float about from place to place. Some little plants even have hairs that wave back and forth and help them move about in the water.

We think of plants as being green. But they are not all green. There are thousands that have no green coloring in them at all. Many of the plants that are too small to be seen without a microscope are colorless. Some bigger plants are, too. Indian pipe is one of them.

For millions of years there were no plants with flowers anywhere on earth. When at last flowering plants appeared, they spread far and wide. There are still many plants without flowers. There are mosses and ferns and horsetails. There are sea-weeds and mushrooms and pine trees. There are others besides. But more than half of all the kinds of plants in the world today have flowers.

SUGAR FACTORIES

THE CORN plant in the picture does not look much like a factory, but it is one. It is a sugar factory. It works from daylight to dark every day, even on Sunday.

The corn plant has to have just two things for making sugar. It must have water and carbon dioxide. The carbon dioxide comes from the air. It is one of the gases the air is made of. The water comes from the ground.

Most of the sugar-making goes on in the leaves of the corn plant. The "machines" are very, very tiny green dots. They can make sugar because they have the almost-magic green dye chlorophyll in them.

The carbon dioxide comes into the leaf through tiny holes in the skin. The water has a longer trip. It first soaks into the roots of the corn plant. It travels through water tubes in the roots and the stem to the leaves.

As soon as water from the ground reaches a leaf it travels all over the leaf through the veins. It finally reaches the tiny green dots. They put the water and carbon dioxide together to make sugar.

Most factories need coal or electricity to make them run. A corn plant runs on sunshine.

A corn plant makes sugar for itself. It has to have food. But a corn plant cannot live on just sugar any better than we could. After it has made sugar, it makes the sugar into other kinds of food it needs.

Corn plants are not the only plants that make sugar. All green plants do. And they are the only true sugar factories. Without green plants there would not be any sugar or any other food for animals to eat. Green plants are the world's most important factories.

Corn

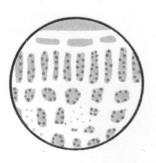

Cells of Green Leaf Greatly Magnified

BEGGAR PLANTS

ALL GREEN PLANTS can make food for themselves. Nearly all those that are not green must get food ready-made. We can call them beggar plants.

All the mushrooms are beggar plants. Some of them grow on living plants and get food from them. Others live on dead plants.

MUSHROOMS

Shaggy Mane

Death Angel

Brownie Cap

Shelf Fungus

Orange-Milk Lactar

Inky Cap

Gypsy

These pictures of mushrooms do not show you the whole plants. Much of every mushroom plant is hidden. The hidden part is made up of tiny threads that grow in the ground or in the wood of old logs or tree trunks. These threads gather up food and water. We see only the spore-bearing stalks that shoot up from the hidden threads. Spores serve mushroom plants as seeds. But they are much, much smaller than seeds.

There are hundreds of kinds of mushrooms. Some of them have beautiful colors. Among the colors are violet, bright yellow, rose, and scarlet.

Some mushrooms are good to eat. But some are deadly poison. It is never safe to eat a mushroom found growing wild unless an expert says that it is a good one. One of the mushrooms in the pictures is very dangerous. It is easy to guess from the name which one it is—the death angel.

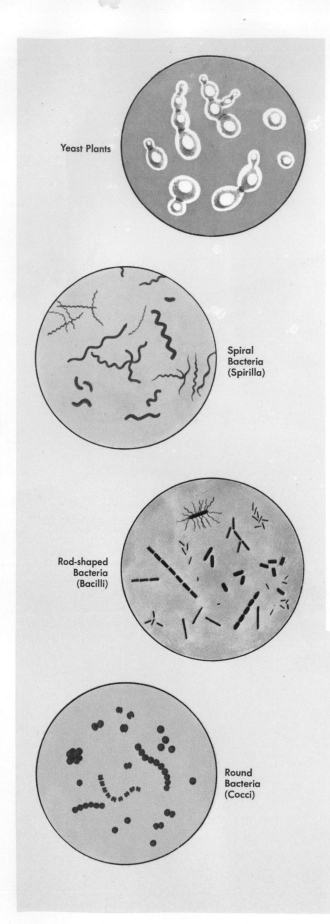

Yeast Plants

Spiral Bacteria (Spirilla)

Rod-shaped Bacteria (Bacilli)

Round Bacteria (Cocci)

The tiny beggar plants we call yeasts live on sugar that green plants have made. These tiny plants are a big help to us. They make bread rise. As they grow they throw away carbon dioxide. The bubbles of this gas make the bread puff up. But yeasts can be a nuisance. They get into fruit juices and make them sour. Yeast plants are so tiny that they can float about in the air. There are always some ready to drop into any fruit juice left uncovered.

Yeasts are far too small to be seen without a microscope. Bacteria, most of which are also beggar plants, are smaller still.

Some bacteria are round. Some are like little rods. Some are twisted. It is hard to see how such tiny plants can be important. But they are. Some do us much harm. Others are our good friends.

Our worst enemies among the bacteria are disease germs. Our best friends are the bacteria that make dead plants and animals decay. If it weren't for them the earth would be a great rubbish heap.

Molds are beggar plants, too. But they are big enough to be seen. They are much like mushroom plants except that they are smaller. Most of us have seen mold growing on bread and oranges. The mold gets from the bread and oranges the food it has to have.

We should not look down on these beggar plants because they get their food from green plants or from animals that eat green plants. We do the same thing ourselves.

Mold on an Orange

Pitcher Plant

Venus's Flytrap

Sundew

Butterwort

PLANTS THAT EAT INSECTS

MANY INSECTS eat plants. Strange as it seems, a few kinds of plants turn the tables and eat insects. These plants cannot go flying about catching insects as birds do. They cannot run about, either. Instead, they have to set traps to catch the insects they eat.

Pitcher plants have leaves that are traps. The leaves, which are like pitchers, hold rain water. Insects crawl into the pitchers and cannot get out. They are drowned. Then the plant uses them as food.

The tiny sundew has sticky hairs on its leaves. When an insect is caught on one of the hairs, other hairs fold in to hold the insect tight until it is digested.

The butterwort has leaves that are sticky all over. The bladderwort, which grows in water, has little hollow balls that are traps.

One of the best traps found anywhere among the plants is on the Venus's flytrap. There is a trap at the end of each leaf. The trap shuts when an insect touches one of the hairs on it. It stays shut until the leaf is ready for another meal.

Most green plants make for themselves all the food that they need. The plants that eat insects live where it is not easy for them to get all the materials they have to have for food-making. They do, therefore, just what we do—they eat some meat.

Bladderwort

Bachelor's-Button   Morning Glory   Zinnia   Petunia   Marigold

FLOWERS WE KNOW

ALL THE FLOWERS in these pictures are well known. Some of them—those on this page—we raise in our gardens. Those on the next page are wild flowers. They grow in our fields and woods and lakes and along our roadsides. No one has to plant them or weed them or water them.

There are thousands and thousands of different kinds of flowers. They are not all showy like these. The flowers of grass and of many trees and of many weeds are very small. They do not have big bright-colored petals. But all flowers help the plants that have them in the same way. They form or help to form seeds to start new plants.

Seeds are formed in the part of the flower called the pistil. Before seeds will form in a pistil, some of the flower dust called pollen must reach the pistil. As a rule the pollen must come from the pollen sacs of another flower. Wind may carry it. But much of it is carried by bees and other insects.

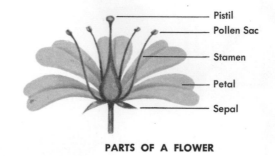

Pistil
Pollen Sac
Stamen
Petal
Sepal

PARTS OF A FLOWER

Flowers get insects to carry pollen for them by offering them food. Many flowers have a sweet juice called nectar. Pollen, too, is good food for some insects. The insects go from flower to flower to find something to eat. As they do they get some pollen on their fuzzy bodies. They rub some of this off on the pistil of the next flower they visit. Most flowers that need the help of insects have bright-colored petals. When it is time for pollen-carrying, these petals wave in the breeze to say,

Columbine

Wild Rose

Violet

Turk's-Cap Lily

Trillium

Lady's Slipper

Trailing Arbutus

American Lotus

"Come, insects. Your dinner is ready." A flower's perfume is a kind of dinner bell, too. If we watch the flowers in our gardens, we are almost sure to see bees and butterflies flying from one to another.

Seed catalogues are fun to look at. Every year there are new kinds of flowers for our gardens. The story of our wild flowers is not so happy. There are not so many wild flowers as there used to be. We have cut down many forests where wild flowers used to grow. We have cut down the wild flowers along our roadsides before they had time to bloom. We have even burned all the plants along some roadsides. And careless people pick too many of the wild flowers that are left. Some of the wild flowers we all know now may disappear if we are not careful. Wild flowers can hold their own with weeds and other plants, but they have no way of protecting themselves from careless people.

Cherries

Cranberries

Plums

Mango

Persimmon

Red Raspberries

Peaches

Strawberries

Lemons

Grapes

Bananas

Banana Plant

FRUITS FROM NEAR AND FAR

EVEN the earliest people probably discovered that some plants have fruits that are sweet and juicy and good to eat. Of course, they could eat only the fruits that grew near by. Today in our fruit markets there are fruits from many different parts of the world. Bananas, for instance, grow only in hot, wet lands. Cranberries are found only in the swampy lands of cool regions.

Apples grow in many parts of the world. They grow in the regions where the cave men lived. Probably the cave men ate many of them. But how different the early apples were from the ones we have now! They were little and hard, like the crab apples we use for jelly. People have found ways of raising better and better apples. Almost all the other fruits we raise are also much bigger and prettier and better tasting than their wild ancestors.

Fruits are packages in which plants pack their seeds. Some, such as plums and peaches, have only one seed in each fruit. Apples and pears have several. Watermelons have hundreds!

Blueberries

Apple

Navel Oranges

Figs

Watermelon

Cranberries

Dried Dates

Date Palm

In the beginning, all fruits had seeds in them. But now there are some seedless fruits. Bananas are almost seedless. The tiny dark specks in a banana are all that is left of seeds the banana once had. No new banana plants would grow from them.

There are also oranges with no seeds at all. These oranges are of no use to the trees that bear them. But they are very good to eat. There are other seedless fruits, too. Pineapples and some kinds of grapes are among them.

Fortunately, many fruit trees and bushes and vines do not have to be raised from seeds. New trees and bushes and vines can be raised from buds or twigs of older plants. Only the first Golden Delicious apple tree, for instance, grew from a seed. Many other Golden Delicious apple trees were raised from twigs of this first tree. They in turn furnished more twigs for more trees. Now there are many Golden Delicious apple trees in our orchards.

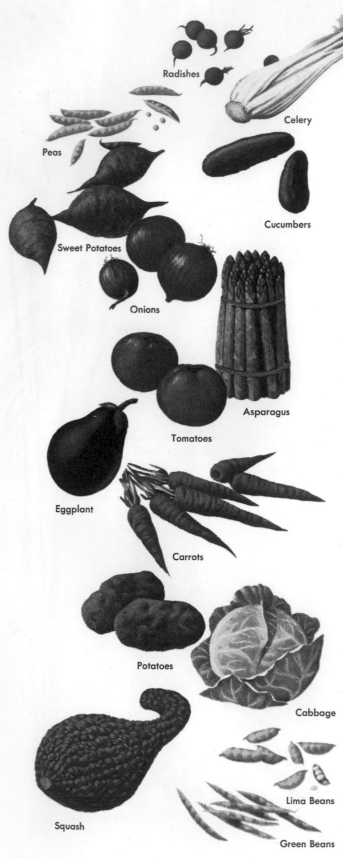

Radishes

Celery

Turnips

Cauliflower

Lettuce

Peas

Cucumbers

Sweet Potatoes

Onions

Asparagus

Tomatoes

Eggplant

Carrots

Potatoes

Cabbage

Lima Beans

Squash

Green Beans

VEGETABLES
IN OUR GARDENS

WHEN A PERSON eats a vegetable, he is eating a part of a plant. But not all vegetables are the same part of the plant. Shelled beans and peas are seeds. A head of cabbage or of lettuce is a bunch of leaves. When we eat asparagus we are eating the stems of asparagus plants. We eat the leaf stalks of celery. A head of cauliflower is made up of flower buds. Carrots, radishes, sweet potatoes, and turnips are roots. A white potato is an underground stem. An onion is a bulb. A tomato has seeds in it. Since it has seeds in it, scientists call it a fruit, even though it is not sweet. Cucumbers, squashes, green beans, and eggplants have seeds and are therefore fruits, too.

A gardener who plants a radish seed knows that he will get only one radish from it. To get the root we eat, we pull up the whole plant. The rule of "one from one" holds for most of the vegetables that are roots. It holds for cabbage, head lettuce, and cauliflower, too.

But when a gardener plants some seeds he expects to get many vegetables from each one. A bean seed, for instance, grows into a big plant. The plant has many flowers on it. And from the flowers come the beans. "Many from one" is the rule for most vegetables that are seeds or fruits.

As a rule a gardener does not raise asparagus and white potatoes from seed. For asparagus he plants asparagus roots. Several stems grow from each set of roots. The roots live in the ground year after year. White potatoes are raised from pieces of potato. Each piece has a bud or eye on it. A potato plant should bear several potatoes.

Robin with Blackberry

SEEDS THAT GO TRAVELING

IF THE seeds of a cattail did not have a good way of traveling, all the cattails would be growing in one spot. But cattail seeds do have a good way of traveling. It is so good that there are cattails in swampy places all over the world.

A cattail seed has a little parachute of down. It can travel a long way on the wind. Milkweed and dandelion seeds and many others have parachutes of down that help them travel through the air.

Some seeds travel through the air on wings instead of with parachutes. Maple and elm seeds have wings.

Many seeds have stickers that catch in the fur of animals. They get free rides to new places. Their stickers have helped the cocklebur and the sticktight to travel far and wide.

Some seeds get free rides in mud that sticks to the feet of birds. Some even ride inside the bodies of birds. A robin, for instance, may swallow a wild blackberry. It digests the soft part of the berry, but the seeds go through the bird's body unharmed.

The seeds of the American lotus float to new places in seed holders that make good boats. Some plants have flat seed pods. If a flat seed pod lands on snow or ice, it can coast along. The seed pod of the black locust is a good coaster.

The seeds of the tumbleweed do not have wings. They do not have parachutes. They do not have stickers. They have no way of floating or coasting. But they travel for miles. When the seeds are ripe the whole plant dries up. The stem breaks off close to the ground, and the whole plant is blown along by the wind, dropping its seeds as it goes.

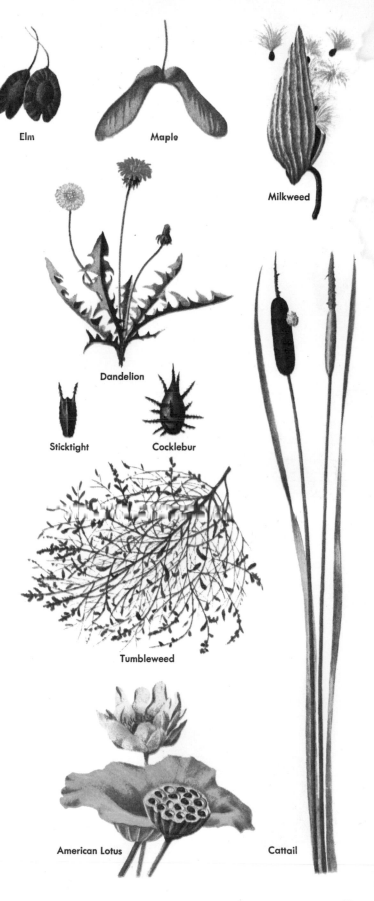
Elm
Maple
Milkweed
Dandelion
Sticktight
Cocklebur
Tumbleweed
American Lotus
Cattail

OUR BODIES

No ONE would have any trouble telling apart the people in the picture. Some are slender, while others are rather fat. Some have light hair; some have dark. Some are men; some are women. But in many, many ways their bodies are alike. All of us are built on very much the same plan.

Our bones make the framework for our bodies. Each one of us has more than 200. All our bones together make up our skeleton.

Every movement of our bodies is carried on by muscles. Some muscles are much larger and thicker than others. But they all work the same way. They stretch and get longer, or shorten and get thicker.

We have to have air, just as all other animals do. We breathe with lungs. Our lungs are built up of many tiny air sacs. Air comes into them through the nose or mouth and the throat.

The food we eat has to be changed to a liquid before it can get to all parts of our bodies. We say that it has to be digested.

The food is first chewed in the mouth. It is mixed with a juice called saliva. From the mouth it goes down a long tube to the stomach. The stomach churns it around and mixes it with another digestive juice. Then it goes to the small intestine. A person's small intestine is about three times as long as he is tall. It is only about as big around as his thumb. Several other juices help digest the food here. One of these juices comes from the liver, another from the pancreas.

By the time the food has made the long trip through the small intestine all of it has been digested that is going to be digested. The part of the food that is not digested goes to the large intestine. It stays there until the muscles in the walls push it out of the body.

Blood goes all over our bodies to carry the supplies that are needed. It carries the part of the air that we need. It also carries digested food.

The heart pushes the blood through the blood vessels. It beats about 70 times a minute day and night. The heart is made of muscle. Every time it beats it is squeezing blood out into the blood vessels.

There are three kinds of blood vessels. Arteries carry blood away from the heart. Veins bring blood back to the heart. Tiny vessels called capillaries carry blood from the arteries to the veins.

Bits of our bodies are always wearing out. Waste materials are always being formed. Our kidneys are very important because they help us get rid of these wastes. The blood picks up wastes and brings them to the kidneys.

The body has a good system for sending messages. Our nerves are its telegraph lines. They carry messages to and from our brains.

Of course, our brains are very, very important. Without them we could not see or hear or smell or feel or taste. Our eyes would not be of any use without a brain to send messages to. We really see with our brains. We also hear and smell and feel and taste with them. Our tongues, noses, ears, and skin are just message senders. We think and remember with our brains, too. Without brains we would not be any better off than a jellyfish.

The skin covers the whole body. It protects the rest of the body from drying up and from being injured. It helps keep germs out.

Our hair is really a part of our skin. So are our nails. No one needs to be told that our skin has a great deal to do with our looks. Imagine not having a skin!

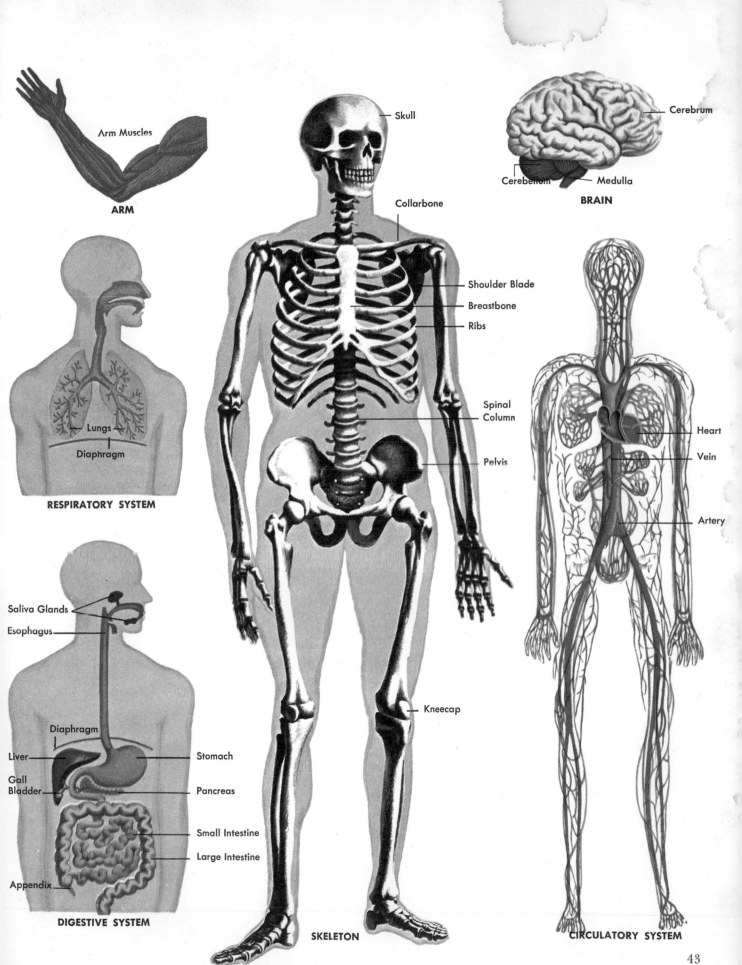

Arm Muscles

ARM

Cerebrum

Cerebellum — Medulla

BRAIN

Skull

Collarbone

Shoulder Blade

Breastbone

Ribs

Spinal Column

Pelvis

Heart

Vein

Artery

Lungs

Diaphragm

RESPIRATORY SYSTEM

Kneecap

CIRCULATORY SYSTEM

Saliva Glands

Esophagus

Diaphragm

Liver

Gall Bladder

Stomach

Pancreas

Small Intestine

Large Intestine

Appendix

DIGESTIVE SYSTEM

SKELETON

THE AIR WE BREATHE

THE AIR round about us is a mixture of different gases. More than three-fourths of it consists of nitrogen. Most of the rest of the air is made up of oxygen. Air also contains small amounts of carbon dioxide, argon, and several other gases.

There is always some water vapor in the air around us. Sometimes there is a great deal. But we do not call water vapor a part of the air. Air would still be air even if all the water vapor were taken out of it.

Oxygen is the part of the air we have to have. When air comes into our lungs, oxygen goes into the tiny blood vessels in our lungs. The blood carries it to all parts of our body.

The blood brings back carbon dioxide from all parts of our body to our lungs. The air we breathe out has much less oxygen in it than it had when we breathed it in. It has much more carbon dioxide in it. But not all the gases change. The nitrogen and the other gases stay just the same. There is more water vapor.

Would it be better for us if the air were all oxygen? Not at all. The scientist who discovered oxygen put a mouse in a bottle of it. The mouse felt very energetic. It ran about so fast that it very soon wore itself out. We would wear ourselves out in a hurry if there weren't any nitrogen to weaken the oxygen.

People have been living on the earth for at least a million years and have been using up oxygen.

Other animals have been using it up, too. So have fires. But there is still plenty of oxygen. The secret is that green plants, when they are making sugar, throw away oxygen. They use up the carbon dioxide we and other animals throw away. We have to thank green plants not only for making food for us but also for keeping the air fit to breathe.

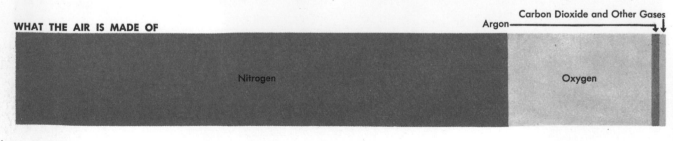

WHAT THE AIR IS MADE OF

Carbon Dioxide and Other Gases

Argon

Nitrogen

Oxygen

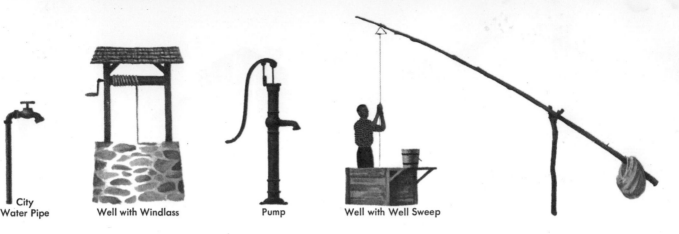

City
Water Pipe

Well with Windlass

Pump

Well with Well Sweep

THE WATER WE DRINK

ALL LIVING THINGS must have water to keep them alive. A human being can live only a few days without it.

It is not hard to understand why our bodies need water. They are made up partly of water. If a person weighs 100 pounds, the water in his body weighs about 60 pounds! We are constantly losing water from our bodies. The amount we lose has to be put back again. Everyone needs about six glasses of water a day.

It is not always easy to get good water to drink. The water of oceans is too salty to drink. Some water is too muddy. Some has so much iron or sulphur in it that it has a bad taste. Even if water is clear and pleasant to drink, it may not be safe. For it may have tiny disease germs in it.

It is not always easy to get enough water, either. Some big cities have to bring water from lakes hundreds of miles away. The water comes in great pipes or channels called aqueducts. In some places big dams have been built across rivers to make the rivers spread out into lakes.

Smaller cities may get their water from wells. Many of the villages of long ago grew up around wells. Many of the families who live in villages and on farms today have their own wells. In some parts of the world water from wells or springs is carried from door to door.

Today most cities purify their water. They make it pleasant and safe. One way of taking mud out of water is to filter it. Layers of sand strain out the particles of mud. One way of making water safe is to add chlorine to it. Chlorine kills germs. One way of taking away unpleasant tastes is to shoot the water high into the air. This way of purifying water is called aeration.

Hoover Dam

THE FOOD WE EAT

EVERY MINUTE of our lives, our hearts are beating and pumping blood through our bodies. Every minute of our lives, we breathe in and out. Most of the time other parts of the body are working, too. It takes energy to keep our body machines going. Of course, the harder we are working or playing, the more energy it takes. All this energy comes from the food we eat. Our food does for us what gasoline does for an automobile.

But our food has to do much more for us than gasoline does for an automobile. It has to furnish the materials we need for mending parts of our bodies that are injured or worn out. It has to give us more of these same materials to make us grow. It would be very queer indeed if gasoline could mend a punctured tire or iron out a dent in a fender. It would be queerer still if gasoline could make a little automobile grow into a big one. Gasoline is for going, not for growing.

We have to have foods for both going and growing. We also have to have foods that make our body machines run smoothly. Food has to do for us what spark plugs and oil do in an automobile.

Getting enough food to keep us from being hungry is not the same as getting the right food. A child who ate nothing but candy would soon be sick even though he might not be hungry. Sugar is a good "go" food, but it isn't a "grow" food at all. And it does not help make our body machines run smoothly.

The pictures show eight groups of foods. To get all that we need from what we eat, we should have something from each of these groups every day.

Milk helps build good muscles and strong teeth and bones. Boys and girls should have a quart of milk a day. They need not drink it all. Some of it may be in ice cream, soup, or cheese.

Eggs are also good grow foods. So are meat, fish, and chicken. Once in a while dried beans or nuts may be used instead of meat.

Potatoes are good go foods. They have starch in them, and starch gives us energy.

Every day we should have two other vegetables besides potato. One should be green or yellow. At least one should be raw. Green and yellow vegetables are rich in minerals and vitamins. These substances are the "sparks" and "oil" that keep our body machines running smoothly. Fruits give us vitamins and minerals, too.

Butter and margarine are go foods. They are mostly fat. They also have certain vitamins in them that are rather scarce in other foods.

Bread and breakfast cereals are good for going and growing and keeping our machines running smoothly. If they are made of whole grains, as they should be, they have in them minerals our bodies must have.

In these pictures there are no cakes or puddings or pies. They are good foods, but we do not have to have them. A good rule is to eat the foods we really need first and then eat these sweets if we still want them.

KEEPING FIT
FOR FUN

No ONE can have very much fun if he is sick. We all want to stay well.

To keep our bodies in good running order, we must have plenty of fresh air to breathe. We must have plenty of good water to drink. We must eat the right kinds of food. But just giving our bodies plenty of air and food and water is not enough to keep them in good running order.

Rest is important. Work and play mean wear and tear on our bodies. While we are working and playing, our bodies are forming waste materials. When a person feels tired, it is because his body is forming waste faster than his blood can carry it away. A person who is tired gets cross easily. He cannot think fast. He is likely to take cold. Everyone must give his body a chance to get rid of the waste and to build up again any bit that is worn out.

Children need more time for resting than grown-up people need. Their bodies not only have to be repaired; they also have to grow. No one's body can easily grow bigger while he is working or playing and wearing it out.

Sleep is the best kind of rest. Not all children need the same amount of sleep. A boy or girl who is still tired when it is time to get up in the morning probably is not getting enough sleep even if he is getting as much as most boys and girls of his age need. Doctors tell us that most children 9 or 10 years old need between 11 and 12 hours of sleep every night. Children 11 years old should have about 11 hours. Twelve-year-olds need a little less.

Our bodies need rest, but some people rest too much. They do not get enough exercise. Not many children need to be told to get more exercise, but a few of them need to play and work harder than they do. Exercise makes muscles strong. It makes the blood rush through the body faster, carrying food and oxygen.

It is good to play out of doors. Exercise is especially good when it is out in fresh air and sunshine.

Keeping ourselves clean is another help in keeping our body machines running smoothly. Of course, we look better, too, when we are clean. A bath every day is a good rule for most of us.

We have to pay special attention to keeping our teeth clean. Teeth that are not brushed often are more likely to decay than clean teeth.

Everyone who owns an automobile has it checked every so often to be sure that it is in good shape. We should have our body machines checked every so often, too. For our check-ups we go to doctors and dentists. Doctors can help us keep from getting sick. Dentists can clean our teeth much better than we can. Of course, if something is wrong, doctors and dentists know what to do. They can make us fit for fun again.

49

Shale

Sandstone

Limestone

Conglomerate

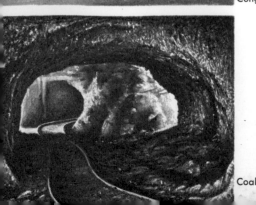

Coal

UNDER OUR FEET

NO MATTER where we are on the earth there is rock below us. Even if we are on a big ship in the middle of the ocean there is rock below us. It is beneath the bottom of the sea.

On land the rock below us is often covered with soil. There was no soil here when the earth was very young. Soil is made mostly of broken-up rock, and the rock had to have time to break up. Now the rock below our feet may be covered by a layer of soil many feet deep.

Even today we see much bare rock. But this rock is not the rock which was at the surface in the beginning. It is much newer.

A great deal of the rock we see is made-over rock. Thinking of a cake may help us understand how rocks are made over. A cook makes a cake. Some of it gets dry and crumbles. The cook takes the bits of cake and makes a pudding of them. In the same way, some rocks are "pudding" made from the "crumbs" of earlier rocks.

Sandstone, shale, and conglomerate are "pudding" rocks. Sandstone is made out of grains of sand. A piece of sandstone feels gritty. Shale is made of mud. The rock particles in mud are smaller than grains of sand. Conglomerate is made mostly of pebbles. Another name for it is pudding stone.

Sandstone, shale, and conglomerate are often called water-made rocks, for as a rule they are made under water. Rivers carry pebbles and sand and mud down to lakes and seas. When the water of a river gets to a lake or sea, it drops its load.

50

As it slows down, first it drops its load of pebbles, then its sand, and finally its mud. On the floor of the lake or sea there come to be thick layers of pebbles and sand and mud. As millions of years go by, these layers are changed into solid rock.

Rocks made at the bottom of a lake or sea do not always stay there. Land and sea change. Much of the dry land of today was once under water. We may find water-made rocks even at the tops of tall mountains.

The plants and animals of long ago helped make some of the rocks under our feet. Coal was made from forests that grew in swamps of long ago. Limestone was made mostly of the shells of animals of the sea.

But water had nothing to do with the making of some of the rock now on the surface of the earth. Granite, which is common, is an igneous rock. "Igneous" comes from a word that means "fire." Igneous rocks are formed from hot, liquid rock that is pushed up from deep down in the earth. Basalt is another common "fire" rock.

After they have been made, rocks may be changed greatly. Limestone may be heated and pressed deep down in the ground until it changes to marble. Shale may be changed to slate. Sandstone may be changed to quartzite. And so it goes.

Rocks that have been greatly changed are called by a long name. They are called metamorphic rocks.

The rocks under our feet are a kind of storybook. From them scientists can read the story of what happened on the earth before there were any people.

Granite

Slate

Basalt

Marble

Soil

Subsoil

Shale

Sandstone

Quartzite

51

PEBBLES

EVERY PEBBLE was once a part of a big mass of rock. It was broken off the big mass of rock in some way. Perhaps a plant grew in a crack and broke it off. Perhaps water froze in a crack. Perhaps waves broke it off by hurling other pebbles against it. There are ever so many different kinds of pebbles because there are ever so many different kinds of rock.

Many of the pebbles we find on beaches are smooth and rather round. But pebbles are never smooth and round to begin with. Most of those that are smooth when we find them have been rolled along by water and have been rubbed against so many other pebbles that their rough edges have been worn away. Some are so waterworn that no one can tell what kind of rock they are without breaking them open. Some pebbles are scoured smooth by windblown sand. These pebbles may have sharp corners.

Many pebbles are pretty, but not many are valuable. Once in a while, however, a really valuable pebble is found. About 100 years ago the children of a farmer in South Africa found a pretty pebble on the bank of a river. It looked like a lump of frosted glass. They played with it for a while and then put it aside. A neighbor saw it and offered to buy it. They told him he could have it for nothing. The pebble turned out to be a big diamond. No one had known before that there are diamonds in South Africa. Now a very large part of all the diamonds in the world comes from there. Most of them are dug from deep mines.

Diorite   Porphyry   Porphyry   Granite   Granite

Granite   Granite   Shale   Shale   Shale

Quartz   Quartz   Quartz   Quartz   Pumice

Limestone   Quartzite   Gneiss   Basalt   Basalt

FOSSILS

Millions of years ago a big animal walked along the edge of a pond. It made deep footprints in the mud there. No other animals walked along and spoiled those footprints. Rain did not wash them away. The mud was covered by more mud. In time the footprints were buried deep in the ground. The mud they were made in became solid rock. They have lasted for millions of years.

Such footprints are called fossils. A fossil is a trace found in rock of some plant or animal of long ago. We would not know about the animals and plants that lived when the earth was young if we had not found fossils of them. Of course, not all fossils are footprints.

A fossil may be a whole animal buried in such a way that its body did not decay. Nearly 50 million years ago many insects were trapped in gum from pine trees. Later some of the gum was buried underground. It became amber. In many pieces of amber there are fossils of insects.

Sabertooth Skeleton

Many fossils are hard parts of plants and animals that have been petrified. "Petrified" means "changed to stone." Suppose a bone is buried in the ground. The water in the ground may dissolve the bone little by little and leave some mineral in its place. At last none of the real bone is left. There is a bone of stone instead. Trunks of trees are petrified in the same way. Petrified wood may be beautiful.

Insect in Amber   Cast of Trilobite

Dinosaur Footprints

Some fossils are bones that were kept from decaying. In the tar pits of California bones of many animals such as sabertooths and mastodons have been found. The tar preserved them.

Some fossils are casts, like the casts children make by pouring plaster into a mold. An animal dies and is covered with mud. Its body decays and leaves a space in the mud. The space is a mold. Mud fills it up. In time the mud hardens into solid rock. Most of what we know about trilobites, the world's leading animals half a billion years ago, comes from studying casts of them.

Petrified Wood

GIANTS
OF LONG AGO

THE ELEPHANT is the biggest animal living on land today. But millions of years ago, back in the Age of Reptiles, there were many much bigger land animals. They were dinosaurs. "Dinosaur" means "terrible reptile." The dinosaurs were not all terrible, but some of them were.

The terrible dinosaurs were meat eaters. The biggest of these meat eaters was *Tyrannosaurus*. This big fellow was three times as tall as a man. It had jaws a yard long and very sharp teeth. Sharp claws helped it catch its prey.

Many of the dinosaurs were plant eaters. Some of the big plant eaters spent most of their time in ponds. They ate the plants that grew in the ponds. Besides, the water helped them hold up their big bodies. *Brontosaurus* was one of the biggest plant-eating dinosaurs. Its name means "thunder reptile." *Brontosaurus* was so big that perhaps it shook the ground when it walked about.

Some dinosaurs had armor. Some had horns. *Triceratops* was one of the horned dinosaurs. Its name means "three horns."

None of the dinosaurs had big brains. They must all have been stupid.

Dinosaurs have long, hard names. They did not have any names when they were alive. There were not any people then to name them. Scientists gave them their names millions of years after the last one died. No one would know anything about these giants of long ago if scientists had not found fossils of them.

Tyrannosaurus

Brontosaurus

Triceratops

54

MOUNTAINS THAT SMOKE

IN MANY PARTS of the world there are mountains that smoke. At times, that is, clouds of smoke rise from them. The smoke may be a danger sign. With a rumble and roar red-hot rock may begin pouring out of the top of the mountain. It may run down the sides of the mountain and bury farms and villages. Bits of rock may be shot high into the air.

The mountains that smoke are called volcanoes. They get their name from Vulcan, the Roman god of fire.

Of one thing we can be sure. Any mountain that smokes built itself. Every volcano begins with a crack that reaches down from the earth's surface to a pocket of red-hot rock deep, deep underground. Some of this hot rock is pushed up through the crack to the top of the ground. It may be pushed up rather slowly. Or there may be explosions that cause earthquakes and shoot bits of rock skyward.

The hot rock that pours out of the opening is called lava. Lava hardens before it has flowed very far. Most of the rock dust shot high in the air falls down near the opening. Around the opening there is the beginning of a mountain.

When a volcano sends out hot rock we say that it is erupting. Every time a volcano erupts, it is likely to become higher.

Every volcano has a great "saucer" at the top. This "saucer" is called a crater.

When a volcano has been quiet for many years, we call it a dead volcano. But no one can ever be sure that a dead volcano will stay dead. No one can be sure that a volcano will never erupt again.

HOW A VOLCANO BUILDS ITSELF

Valley Glacier

RIVERS OF ICE

THE PICTURE shows a river of ice moving down a valley. Another name for a river of ice is "valley glacier." There are valley glaciers in the mountains in many parts of the world. One of our country's famous parks is named Glacier National Park because there are many glaciers in its mountains.

A valley glacier begins with a snowfield. The snow becomes ice, and the ice starts to move. Of course, the ice in a river of ice does not move fast like the water in an ordinary river. It may move only a few inches a day.

Deep Crevasse

Most valleys are not straight, and their floors are not smooth. As the ice moves down them, it has to turn and twist and go over humps and hollows. Great cracks come in it. They are called crevasses. Exploring a glacier is dangerous. There is always a chance of falling into a crevasse.

If a river of ice finally comes to a lake or a sea, chunks of it break off. They become icebergs and float away. They can float because ice is lighter than water.

But many rivers of ice never reach a lake or sea. As a glacier moves down a valley it is likely to come to a place warm enough to make the ice melt. The ice may melt back as fast as it is pushed forward. The river of ice then seems to be standing still.

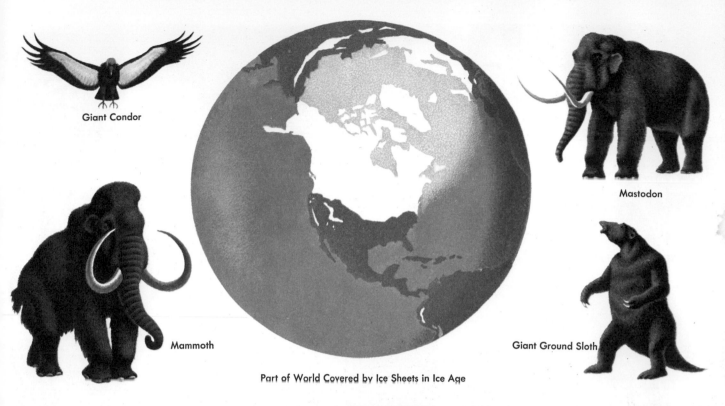

Giant Condor

Mastodon

Mammoth

Giant Ground Sloth

Part of World Covered by Ice Sheets in Ice Age

THE GREAT ICE AGE

BETWEEN a million and two million years ago a great change of climate took place in the northern part of the world. It grew much colder. A great deal of snow fell in the long winters. The summers were not long enough or warm enough to make all the snow melt. In the Far North the snow piled up and up and up. Great sheets of ice formed from the piled-up snow. They grew to be thousands of feet thick.

These great sheets of ice began to spread southward. The ice moved with tremendous force. It shoved soil ahead of it like a giant plow. It cut off the tops of hills it moved over. It gouged out great hollows where there had been little hollows before. It would have ruined towns and cities if there had been any towns and cities to ruin.

Of course, the ice killed the plants it covered. Most animals could move away from it, for the ice did not move fast. It took years for the edge to move forward a mile.

Some of the animals of the time had great hairy coats that helped protect them from the cold. They could live close to the ice.

After some 100 thousand years, warm weather came again. The ice began to melt back. The climate was mild for hundreds of centuries. Then it changed once more and the ice moved forward. For more than a million years the edge of the ice moved backward and forward.

Perhaps the ice age is not yet over. Some scientists think that the ice will come again. But it will not come for at least thousands of years.

Giant Bison

Glyptodont

Sabertooth

FAIRYLANDS UNDERGROUND

WHEN IT RAINS, some of the water sinks into the ground. It sinks into the soil. It may even sink into the rock below. For many kinds of solid rock are not nearly so solid as they seem to be. There are spaces between the particles of rock. Rocks with spaces in them are called porous.

Limestone is one of the porous rocks. Water can sink into limestone easily. It can even travel from place to place through a layer of limestone.

The water that sinks down into the ground is not pure. It has gathered up materials from the air and the soil. Pure water cannot dissolve limestone. But one of the materials water gathers up helps it dissolve limestone. The water that reaches a layer of limestone may dissolve enough of the rock to leave a cavern underground. There are limestone caverns in many parts of the world. A limestone cavern may be very beautiful. It may be like a fairyland.

In a limestone cavern there are often rock "icicles" hanging from the ceiling. They are called stalactites. There are also upside-down rock "icicles" rising from the floor. They are called stalagmites. These rock "icicles" are made by the dripping of water from the ceiling of the cavern. The water evaporates and leaves behind the lime it had in it.

Mammoth Cave and Carlsbad Caverns are among the most famous limestone caverns in our country. They are worth going a long way to see.

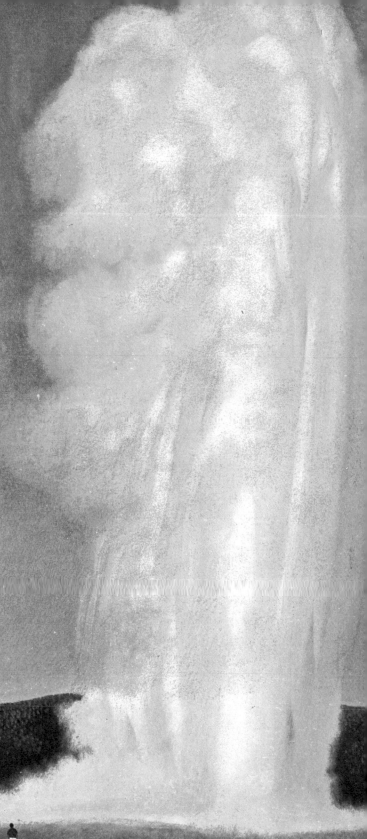

OLD FAITHFUL

OLD FAITHFUL is a famous geyser. It is in Yellowstone National Park, where most of the world's geysers are found.

A geyser is like a hot spring except that the water shoots high into the air when it comes out of the ground. A geyser does not flow all the time. When water shoots up from one, we say that the geyser is erupting. A geyser is always quiet for a time after it erupts.

Old Faithful got its name because it erupts at a regular time. This geyser was first seen by white men in 1870. Since then it has erupted every 65 minutes or so. Visitors seldom have to wait more than an hour to see Old Faithful perform.

When it is time for an eruption, there is a deep rumble. There is a hissing, too. Then up shoots the water. It may go as high as a 12-story building. An eruption lasts about four minutes. This same thing has happened at least half a million times.

Old Faithful, and every other geyser, too, works in this way: There is some hot rock not far below the surface of the ground. A narrow, crooked passage leads down into this hot rock. Water fills up the passage. The water at the bottom gets so hot that it begins to turn to steam. The water in the passage bottles up the steam. But at last the steam pushes with enough force to shoot out the water above it. Before there can be another eruption the passage must fill with water again and the water at the bottom must get boiling hot.

GRAND CANYON

THE GRAND CANYON is the valley of the Colorado River. It is in Arizona. The valley is called a canyon because it has very steep sides. It is easy to see from the picture why it is called grand. It is about a mile deep.

Many people think that the Grand Canyon is the most beautiful sight in America. The soft colors of the rocks in its walls help make it beautiful.

On the rim of the canyon there might very well be a sign saying, "This shows what water can do." For the canyon was made by the river that flows in it. The river had some tools to work with. These tools were sand and gravel. With them it wore away the rock it flowed over.

The walls of the canyon tell a story. The rocks are in layers like the layers in a cake. Many of the layers are sandstone. Others are limestone. Still others are shale. The layers of sandstone and limestone and shale show that this part of the earth was under water for millions and millions of years. Fossils found in them tell about the plants and animals that lived in the region in past ages. The oldest fossils are of plants that lived more than half a billion years ago.

The river has cut its way down through all the layers of limestone and sandstone and shale. Now it has reached a layer of granite. The lowest part of the canyon is sometimes called the Granite Gorge. Granite is a very hard rock. It is so hard that the river is cutting slowly now.

NIAGARA FALLS

WHEN A RIVER comes to a cliff, it falls over. There is nothing else for it to do. Then we have a waterfall. There are hundreds of waterfalls in the world. But none of them is more beautiful than Niagara Falls. Some are much higher, but very few have as much water falling over them.

Niagara is different from most waterfalls because it is in two parts. Goat Island divides it.

This beautiful waterfall was not always divided into two parts. Back in the great ice age the whole northern part of North America was covered with ice. When the ice melted away the Niagara River began carrying water from Lake Erie into Lake Ontario. The river found a great cliff in its way and fell over it. But the cliff was not where the falls are now. It was several miles down the river. There was no island in the river there.

The rock at the top of the cliff was hard. But under it there was softer rock. As the water fell over the cliff it splashed up against this softer rock. It began to wear it away. Little by little the hard rock at the top broke off as the rock was worn away from under it. The waterfall began to move back. It moved back till it came to Goat Island. Then it became two falls instead of one.

Many thousands of people visit Niagara Falls every year. Visitors who see the falls on a sunshiny day often see a rainbow in the mist that comes up from the splashing water.

How Niagara Falls Worked Its Way Backward

Exosphere

Ionosphere

Stratosphere

Troposphere

ABOVE OUR HEADS

THE AIR is a part of the earth. The earth carries its air around with it everywhere it goes.

We can think of the air as a kind of ocean with us at the bottom of it. It reaches high above us, perhaps for more than 600 miles. But high above the ground the particles of air are very far apart. We say that the air is thin. Even at the top of a mountain three miles high the air is so thin that many people have trouble breathing.

Scientists have found out that there are different layers of air. The bottom layer is the troposphere. It is about eight miles deep. Above it is the stratosphere. It is about 40 miles deep. Stretching above the stratosphere for more than 100 miles is the ionosphere. Still higher is the exosphere—the outermost layer of our ocean of air.

The troposphere is the layer of changing weather. In the stratosphere and the layers above it there are no clouds or storms. The air is so thin that the sky is nearly black. In the lower part of the stratosphere the air is very, very cold. But at some higher levels it is hot.

The shooting stars we sometimes see are chiefly in the ionosphere. They are tiny bits of rock that have fallen into our air. Even though the air in the ionosphere is very thin, the bits of rock become white-hot as they fall through it. We must look up into the ionosphere to see the beautiful northern lights, too. In the exosphere the air is even thinner than in the ionosphere.

We have learned much of what we know about our ocean of air from instruments carried high above the earth's surface by unmanned balloons and rockets. But by now men, too, have gone in balloons, rocket planes, and space capsules high into the upper layers of air.

A bucketful of air weighs very little. It would take about 800 bucketfuls of air to weigh as much as one bucketful of water. But the ocean of air is so deep that there is an enormous amount above our heads. It is pushing down on us with a great deal of force. We do not feel the pressure of the air because we are used to it. And we are not mashed partly because there is air all around us.

HIGHER STILL

THE CLOUDS that float above our heads are floating about in our ocean of air. The airplanes that fly above us are flying in the air. So are the birds. Skywriting is always in the air, too. But we can see high above the top of our ocean of air. We can look far out into space.

People of long ago believed that the earth was flat and that the sky was a great blue bowl turned upside down over it. Now we know that the blue of the sky is caused by the air. The air scatters the sunlight and lets more blue light reach our eyes than any other color. Up above our ocean of air the sky would be velvet-black.

What do we see when we look out beyond our ocean of air? In the daytime we see the sun and sometimes the moon, looking very pale. Sunlight is so bright that it blots out almost everything else. But at night we are looking away from the sun. It is easier for us to see far out into space in the clear, dark night sky.

At night the moon looks brighter than in the daytime. At night the Milky Way stretches across the sky. The Milky Way is the light from millions of stars very, very far out in space. We see many separate stars, too. We also see some "stars" that are not really stars. They are planets that travel around the sun just as the earth does. Once in a while a comet is in view. A comet is a great glowing ball with a tail streaming out behind it. People used to be very much afraid of comets. But comets are nothing to be afraid of. Not very long ago the earth actually went through the tail of a comet and was not hurt at all.

Telescopes show us much more in the sky than we can see with our eyes alone. They show us other planets. They show us, too, hundreds of tiny asteroids that circle the sun just as the planets do. With telescopes we find that most of the planets have moons. With them we see countless stars that cannot be seen without their help.

Even with telescopes we cannot see the meteors that are out in space. We see them only when they fall into our air and become shooting stars or, if they are big, fireballs.

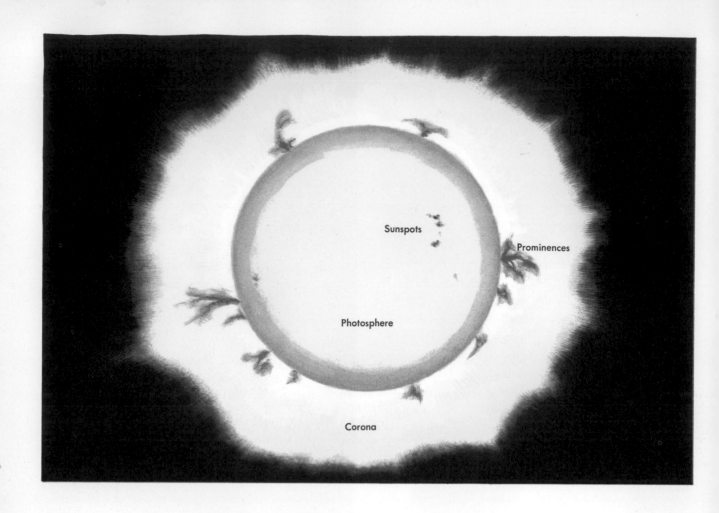

Sunspots
Prominences
Photosphere
Corona

THE SUN

LONG AGO many people worshiped the sun. It is no wonder, for even early people could see that the sun gives the earth light and heat. If it were not for the sun, the earth would be very, very, very cold and very, very, very dark. Not a single plant or animal could live on it.

The sun is an enormous ball of glowing gas. It is so bright that no one should look at it without protecting his eyes. Pictures of the sun show that there are some darker spots on its surface. They are called sunspots. Sunspots move. They are really great storms. In a picture these sunspots look dark. They are not really dark. They are just not quite so bright as the rest of the sun's surface. Sunspots are big enough to swallow up the earth.

Shooting up from the sun there are great streamers of glowing gas called prominences. Some of them go up many, many thousands of miles.

Once in a while the moon comes between the earth and the sun and shuts off our view of the main part of the sun. We say that there is an eclipse of the sun. In an eclipse, a part of the sun that does not usually show comes into sight. This is the sun's corona. It is not so bright as the main part of the sun. It glows with a pale light. Sometimes it is called the sun's halo.

Eclipse of Sun

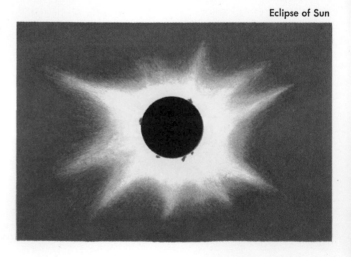

THE PLANETS

THE SUN has a family of at least nine planets. It may have even more. It may have some that are so far away that no one has seen them yet. The farthest planet we know about was not discovered until about 35 years ago. This planet is Pluto. It cannot be seen except with a powerful telescope.

Every planet has its own path around the sun just as our own planet, the earth, has. There is no danger that one planet will bump into another, for the paths of the planets are millions of miles from one another.

Some of our sister planets we see often. They shine in the sky like bright stars. But they do not really give off any light of their own. They shine because the sun is shining on them.

Two planets, Mercury and Venus, have paths closer to the sun than our path. The paths of the other planets are all farther away.

Earth Compared in Size with Sun

Earth

Saturn with Six of Its Nine Moons

Mars with Its Two Moons

Jupiter with Two of Its Twelve Moons

Jupiter is the biggest of the planets. If it were hollow, there would be room for a thousand earths inside it. Through a telescope great streaks and spots show on its surface. Without a telescope it looks like a very bright star.

Saturn is next biggest. This giant planet has beautiful rings around it. The rings do not show without a telescope. To our eyes alone Saturn, too, looks like a very bright star.

Neptune and Uranus are both giants. But they are too far away to be seen without a telescope.

The other planets—Mercury, Mars, Venus, and Pluto—are smaller than the earth. Mercury stays so close to the sun that not many people ever see it. It is lost in the bright light of the sun. Pluto is too far away. Mars and Venus, on the other hand, are common sights. They are close enough to us to be very bright when they are in the right places on their paths to be seen.

Venus is bright partly because it is covered with thick clouds. They throw back most of the sunlight that falls on them. No one has ever been able to see through these clouds.

Mars has white caps at its poles. These caps are probably frost. This planet is dull red, with greenish streaks. The streaks may be plants, and the red sections desert.

Could people like us live on any of the other planets? The answer, scientists think, is no. Most of the planets are either far, far too hot or far, far too cold. Besides, none of them, so far as we can tell, has air like ours.

Crescent Moon   Half-Moon   Full Moon

THE MOON

THE FULL MOON looks like a pale sun when we see it in the sky. But it is really not like the sun at all. It is not a great glowing ball of gas. Instead it is made of solid rock, and it is not glowing. It shines only because the sun is shining on it.

The moon looks as big as the sun. But it is really very, very much smaller. It looks big because it is rather close to us. It is only about 235,000 miles away. The moon is small even compared with the earth—it would take so many to make a ball as big as the earth.

The moon travels around the earth while the earth is traveling around the sun. But as the moon travels around the earth it always keeps the same side toward us.

This side of the moon is not evenly bright all over. Big, rather dark areas make the eyes and nose and mouth of the "man in the moon." Scientists used to think that these darker spots were seas. Now they know that they are great plains. But on maps they are still called seas. The very bright areas are hills and mountains.

Scattered over the part of the moon we see are great hollows, or craters. They look like the craters of volcanoes, but they are much bigger than any craters on earth. They are a real puzzle.

We now know that the far side of the moon also has craters, mountains, and "seas." In 1959 the rocket Lunik III carried a camera beyond the moon and sent back the first pictures of the far side.

The moon would not be a pleasant place to visit. There is no air there, or at least not enough to count. There is no water. In the sunshine it is far too hot for us, and in the shade it is far too cold. No plants and animals live there. People often call it a dead world.

The Earth in the Moon's Sky

The moon does not always look big and round. Sometimes it is a thin crescent. Sometimes it looks like only half a moon. It seems to get bigger and bigger night after night until it is full. Then it seems to get smaller and smaller until no one can see it at all. The different shapes of the moon as we see it are called its phases.

Long ago people made up stories to tell why the moon changed its shape. One story told that moon after moon grew big and round in the sky. As soon as each moon was full, a dragon began taking bites of it. He nibbled at it till he ate it all up.

Of course, this story is foolish. The true story is this: The moon is always round. But we cannot see any of the moon that the sun is not shining on. When the moon is between the earth and the sun, the sun cannot shine on the side toward us. We cannot see the moon at all. But, as the moon travels around the earth, the sun shines on more and more of the side toward us. The moon, we say, is waxing. When it has gone a quarter of its way around, it looks like a half-moon. When it is halfway around, the sun shines on all the side toward us. The moon is full. From then on less and less of the side toward us is lighted up. We say that the moon is waning. Finally the moon disappears.

It is about a month from one full moon to another. For it takes the moon just about a month to travel around the earth. Our word "month" comes from "moon." The pictures on this page show how the moon in the course of a month seems to change shape. They show, too, that the times at which the moon rises and sets change along with its looks.

PHASES OF THE MOON

Young Crescent in the West Just after Sunset

First Quarter Moon in the West Late in the Evening

Nearly Full Moon in the East Early in the Evening

Full Moon in the East Just after Sunset

Waning Moon in the East Late in the Evening

Last Quarter Moon in the East at Midnight

Old Crescent in the East Just before Sunrise

New Moon, Not Visible at All

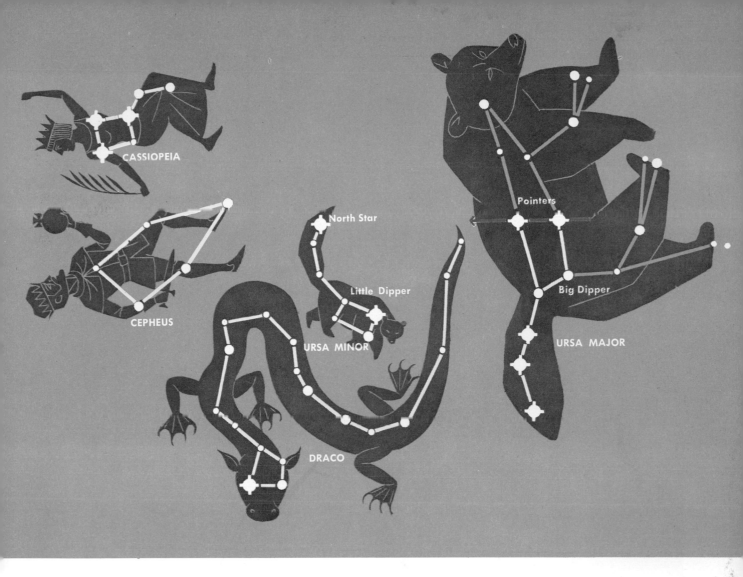

STARS

STARS ARE suns. They are great glowing balls of gas like our sun. But they are not all single suns. Many are double. They are made up of two suns that travel around and around each other. They are so far away that we see the two as one. A star may be two double suns. Some stars are even made of six suns traveling around one another.

The very nearest star is much farther away than our own sun. Suppose that with magic boots a boy could get from the earth to the sun in a single step. It would take him a quarter of a million steps to reach the nearest star.

There are so many stars that it almost makes a person dizzy to think of them. Probably there are as many as there are grains of sand on all our seashores. But most of the stars are so far away that we cannot see them without a telescope. On a clear night a person can see only about 3,000 stars when he looks up at the sky.

The stars we can see with our eyes alone are not scattered evenly over the sky. They are in groups. Scientists call these groups constellations. "Constellation" means "stars together."

To the people of long ago each group of stars made a picture of something. The names of the constellations tell what pictures some of the people of long ago saw in the sky.

The star map above shows some of the constellations we see in our northern sky. It shows, too, the pictures these stars are supposed to make. The North Star, as the picture shows, is in the tail of Ursa Minor, the Little Bear.

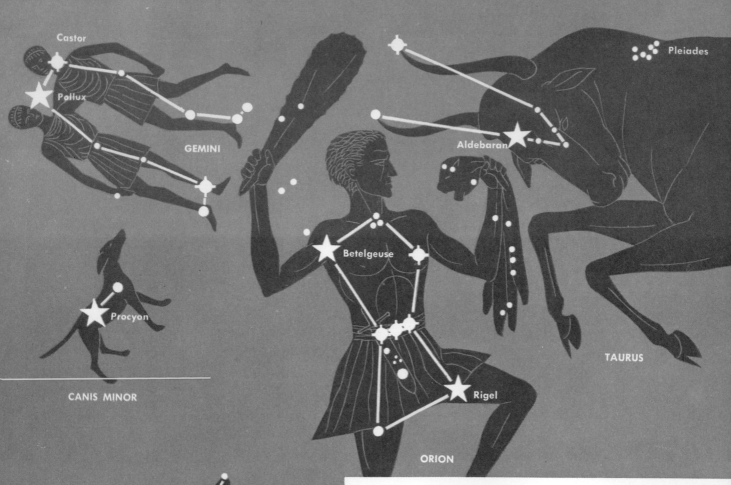

Castor

Pollux

GEMINI

Pleiades

Aldebaran

Betelgeuse

Procyon

CANIS MINOR

Rigel

TAURUS

ORION

Sirius

CANIS MAJOR

The star map on this page shows some of the constellations in our southern sky. In our southern sky we do not see the same groups of stars all year long. The southern sky changes because of the journey of the earth around the sun. We do see many of the northern constellations all year long. We see them year in and year out because the north pole of the earth is always pointed toward the North Star. When we look north in the sky we are always looking toward the constellations near the North Star.

The southern constellations in this sky map can be seen in winter. Some of the brightest stars in the sky are in these constellations. The Dog Star, in Canis Major, the Big Dog, is the brightest of all the stars. Another name for this star is Sirius. Sirius is bright partly because it is rather close to us as sky distances go. The Pleiades are not very bright. But they are easy to find in the sky.

WEATHER, WEATHER EVERYWHERE

EVERY DAY on radio and television weathermen tell us about the weather. Once in a while one will say, "There is no weather in sight." He does not really mean what he says. He really means that there is no change in the weather in sight. There is always weather. No one can get away from it. But different places have different kinds of weather. And the weather in one place may change a very great deal from day to day.

Describing the weather means telling six things:
How hot or cold is it?
Is the sky clear or cloudy?
Is any rain or snow falling?
How much water is there in the air?
How strong is the wind?
From what direction is it coming?

We talk a great deal about the weather. No wonder, for it is very important. Bad weather may spoil our crops, make traveling hard, ruin ball games and picnics, and start forest fires. It may even make people sick or tear down houses.

Inside our buildings we can have about the kind of weather we want. We can take water out of the air or put it in. We can turn on fans to make a breeze. We can start a fire in the furnace. Or we can cool the air. But we cannot do much about the weather out of doors. Scientists have done a little about changing the weather. They have made rain and snow fall from clouds that were passing by. But so far they have not been able to do much. We have to take the weather as it comes, whether it is good or bad.

Cumulus Clouds

CLOUDS

Clouds are an important part of the weather. There are many different kinds. They are all made of either tiny drops of water or tiny bits of ice.

The pictures show some common kinds of clouds. It is easy to tell these clouds when you see them in the sky.

"Cirrus" means "curl." Cirrus clouds are beautiful and feathery. They are made of tiny bits of

Cirrus Clouds

ice. Even those we see in summertime are made of ice. They are always high above the earth. We never get any rain or snow from cirrus clouds.

Cumulus clouds are big and white and fluffy. The word "cumulus" means "pile." Clouds of this kind often tower up so far that they look like fairy castles in the sky. Cumulus clouds are some-

times called fair-weather clouds. They do not give us any rain or snow. But if a cumulus cloud keeps getting bigger and bigger it may turn into a dark thunderhead. We are likely to get rain and thunder and lightning from a thunderhead.

Stratus clouds are all-over clouds. They are gray clouds that may spread over the whole sky. "Stratus" means "layer." Stratus clouds are made

Thunderhead

of bits of ice or drops of water. We may get snow or rain from them.

Airplanes often fly right through clouds. And a great many people, even if they have never flown, have been in clouds. For a fog is simply a cloud that is close to the ground. Fogs are dangerous because it is hard to see through them.

Stratus Clouds

Hurricane

STORMS

Weather can be very pleasant. But stormy weather can be frightening.

Thunderstorms are our commonest storms. They get their name from the lightning and thunder that go with them. During a thunderstorm there are usually some strong gusts of wind. Often there is a heavy shower. Most thunderstorms last for only a few minutes. They are rather small,

Thunderstorm

too. One part of a city may have a thunderstorm while the rest of the city has fair weather.

A tornado is a violent windstorm. It also is small, but it does much more damage than a thunderstorm. The wind is much stronger. Tornadoes are often called "twisters." There is a good reason why. The wind in a tornado whirls around very

fast. It whirls a great deal of dirt up into its cloud. The dirt lets us see the whirl of air. It looks like a funnel. Tornadoes move fast. At one place a tornado lasts only about half a minute. Thunderstorms and tornadoes are summer storms.

Hurricanes are violent windstorms, too. But they are much bigger than tornadoes, and they last much longer. A hurricane may last in one place

Tornado

for a whole day. Hurricanes start over the oceans. As a rule they never travel far inland. Hurricanes come in the late summer and fall.

Ice storms may be truly beautiful. They come when it is just cold enough to make raindrops freeze as they strike. Blizzards are winter storms. They are snowstorms with strong winds.

Ice Storm

Snowstorm

73

WHAT WILL THE WEATHER BE?

BEING A WEATHERMAN on the moon would be easy. For day after day the weather there is just the same—fair and hot in the daytime and fair and cold at night. But the work of a weatherman here is not easy. A weatherman needs many instruments to help him tell about the weather. The pictures show some of the weatherman's helpers.

Thermometers tell how hot or how cold it is. An alcohol thermometer has a glass tube that swells out into a bulb at one end. The bulb is full of colored alcohol. Alcohol can help tell temperature because it expands, or gets bigger, when it is heated, and contracts, or gets smaller, when it is cooled. When it expands, it rises in the tube. There is nowhere else for it to go. When it contracts, it goes lower in the tube. A mercury thermometer works the same way.

The weatherman also has some special kinds of thermometers. One has a pen that writes a record of the temperature.

A barometer measures air pressure. The air is always pressing down with a great deal of force, but sometimes it presses harder than at other times. The air pressure keeps changing. From the way the air pressure is changing the weatherman can tell which way the wind will be blowing. And wind makes a great deal of difference with the weather. "Every wind has its weather" is an old saying and a good one. Some winds are warm; some are cold. Some bring much moisture; others are dry. Some are likely to bring storms.

The round barometer in the picture has a little airtight box inside it. The harder the air is pushing, the more the sides of the little box are pushed in. The black hand of the barometer is fastened to the box. It moves whenever the sides of the box go in or out. The red hand is just a marker.

A weatherman usually has several barometers. He is sure to have a mercury barometer and one that keeps a record of the air pressure.

A barometer helps the weatherman tell what the winds are going to be. A weather vane, or wind vane, tells about the wind right now. It shows from what direction the wind is blowing. The wind makes a weather vane point in the direction from which the wind is coming.

The instrument with cups tells how fast the wind is blowing. Its long name, anemometer, means "wind measure."

A rain gauge measures the rain that falls. If the weatherman tells us that we have had a one-inch rain, he means that enough water fell to make a layer of water an inch thick on the ground.

The balloon is a weather balloon. It carries instruments up high above the earth so that the weatherman will know about the weather there. Knowing about the weather there will help him tell what the weather here is going to be.

A weatherman has still other instruments. One helps him find out how much water there is in the air. Another tells him how many hours of the day the sun has been shining. Still another shows him how high the lowest clouds are.

Even with all his instruments to help him, the weatherman sometimes makes mistakes. But he is right so much of the time that he is a big help.

Anemometer

Weather
Balloon

Alcohol
Thermometer

Wind Vane

Recording Thermometer

Aneroid Barometer

28 29 30 31 27 26

Mercury
Barometer

Rain Gauge

Recording
Barometer

Lever

Pulley

Wedge

Inclined Plane

Wheel and Axle

Screw

Lever

HELP WITH OUR WORK

WE ARE AHEAD of all other animals partly because we have better brains. We are ahead partly because we have good hands. With our good hands we have been able to build machines and use them. We have been able to make work much easier.

People used machines long before they knew there were any such things. A cave man, when he used a small log to pry loose a stone for the door of his cave, was using a machine. He was using a lever. When he skinned a cave bear or split a log with a sharp piece of flint, he was using a machine, too. His piece of flint was a wedge.

The lever and the wedge are two of the machines we call simple machines. There are four other kinds of simple machines: the inclined plane, the screw, the pulley, and the wheel and axle.

Some simple machines help us by letting us move a heavy load without using very much force. The man rolling the barrel up into the truck might not be able to lift the barrel at all. But he can roll it up the slope easily.

Some machines help us by letting us move something much faster than we could move it all by ourselves. If the boy moves his end of the fishing pole just a little, he will jerk the fish he catches high out of the water.

Some machines help us by letting us lift something up by pulling down. With a pulley like the one in the picture a person can raise a flag high above his head by pulling down on the rope.

Many of the machines we use we call tools. Some of our tools are made up of more than one machine. A pair of metal shears, for instance, is made up of two levers and two wedges.

Knowing about the six simple machines helps us to understand complicated machines. For in every big piece of machinery there is at least one simple machine.

For a long, long time all machines were hand-power machines. But after many thousands of years people found out that they did not have to do all their work themselves. They found that some of their tamed animals could help them. They found

they could harness the wind by building windmills. They found they could harness running water by building water wheels. They discovered ways of using heat to run engines. Today much of the work of the world is done with engines.

The big locomotive pictured is driven by a steam engine. To understand how a steam engine works, we have to know that steam takes up ever and ever so much more room than the water it comes from. The idea of a steam engine is this: Water is put in a boiler and is heated until it boils. The steam that is formed pushes its way out through an opening. A piston is put in its path. The steam pushes the piston. The piston turns a wheel, and this wheel turns other wheels.

Boiler   Firebox

630

Piston

STEAM LOCOMOTIVE

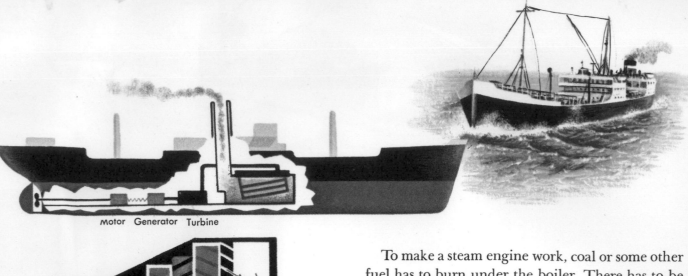

Motor   Generator   Turbine

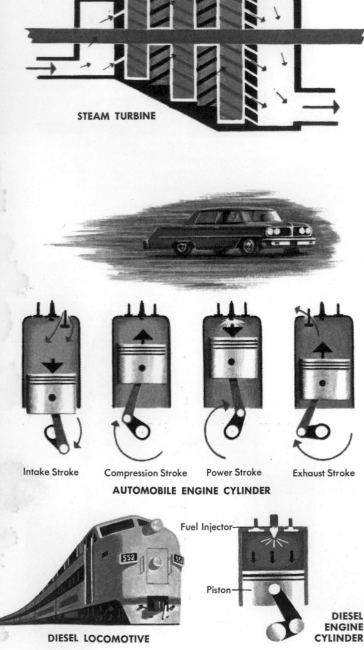

STEAM TURBINE

Intake Stroke   Compression Stroke   Power Stroke   Exhaust Stroke

AUTOMOBILE ENGINE CYLINDER

DIESEL LOCOMOTIVE

Fuel Injector

Piston

DIESEL ENGINE CYLINDER

To make a steam engine work, coal or some other fuel has to burn under the boiler. There has to be oxygen to make the fuel burn. The oxygen comes from the air around the fire.

In another kind of engine run by steam, a jet of steam from the boiler strikes a wheel with blades on it and makes it whirl around. An engine of this kind is called a steam turbine. There are steam turbines in many ships and in many electric power plants. On a ship a steam turbine may turn the ship's propeller. Or it may drive a generator which sends a current of electricity to an electric motor. The motor then turns the ship's propeller.

In the engines in our automobiles the fuel burns *inside* the engine in round metal "boxes" called cylinders. The fuel is gasoline. It burns so fast that we say it explodes. In each cylinder there is a piston. The explosions of the gas make the pistons move, and they make the wheels of the car turn. The gasoline has to have air mixed with it or it will not explode. A spark of electricity sets fire to the mixture.

Not all engines of this kind are in automobiles. Many small engines that work this way help people mow grass and do other kinds of work. Many airplanes have engines of this kind. The engines turn the propellers of the planes.

Many of the locomotives that pull our trains today have diesel engines in them. In many ways a diesel engine is like an automobile engine. Gasoline or oil explodes in each cylinder and pushes a piston. The big difference is that the fuel is not set to burning with a spark. Instead, the air needed is first squeezed until it gets very hot. As soon as a bit of fuel is squirted in, it explodes. Not all diesel engines are in locomotives. Some big trucks and big boats have diesel engines.

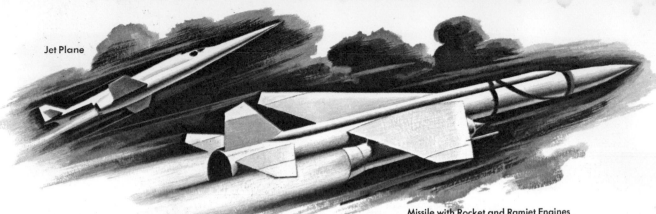

Jet Plane

Missile with Rocket and Ramjet Engines

Gas turbines are much like steam turbines. Jets of hot gas from burning fuel strike the blades of the turbine wheels and make them turn.

Many of the big airplanes of today have jet engines. Fuel burns inside a jet engine just as in automobile and diesel engines. But there is no piston for the gas from the exploding fuel to push. The whole engine moves forward as a jet of hot gas shoots out at the back of the engine.

The simplest jet engine is the ramjet. The air needed to make the fuel burn comes in at the front of the engine. An electric spark starts the fuel to burning. The earliest jet planes had ramjet engines. They were often called "flying stovepipes." A flying stovepipe had to be pushed or towed at the start. It could not take off by itself because it could not get enough air inside it until it was going very fast.

Most of today's jet engines are turbojets. In a turbojet the escaping gas turns a gas turbine. The turbine works a blower at the front of the engine. The blower compresses air from the outside and forces it into the combustion chamber. A turbojet plane can take off from the ground even with a heavy load. The gas turbines of turboprop engines turn propellers as well as blowers.

A rocket engine, like a jet engine, is pushed forward as hot gas from burning fuel shoots out a nozzle at the back of the engine. But there is one big difference between a jet engine and a rocket engine. A jet engine must have air; a rocket engine carries with it the oxygen needed to make its fuel burn. The fuel used in a rocket engine may be a liquid such as alcohol or kerosene. The oxygen is liquid, too. The fuel may instead be a solid fuel which has a chemical containing oxygen mixed with it.

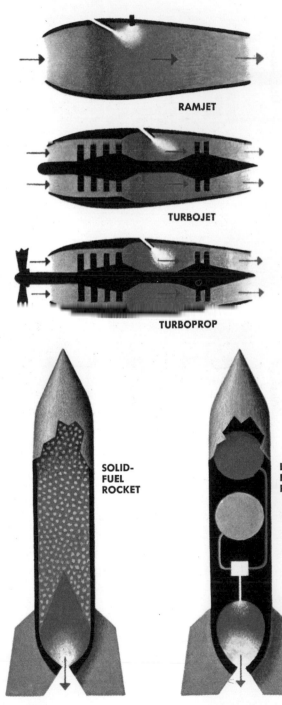

RAMJET

TURBOJET

TURBOPROP

SOLID-FUEL ROCKET

LIQUID-FUEL ROCKET

The big advantage of rocket engines is that they will work up where the air is very thin or even where there is no air at all. They have made space exploration possible.

Rocket engines are used in rocket planes as well as in rockets. A rocket plane has gone faster and higher than any other plane.

Rocket engines would not be nearly so useful in exploring space if multistage rockets had not been invented. A multistage rocket is made up of two or more rockets piled one on top of another. The lowest rocket engine, the first stage, fires. It lifts the rocket to a certain height. As soon as its fuel has been used up, it breaks away and falls back to the ground. The second stage fires and boosts the rocket higher. If there is a third stage, it then fires and gives the rocket another boost, and so on. A multistage rocket may carry scientific instruments or a warhead or an artificial satellite as its payload. The rocket in the illustration is about to put an artificial satellite into orbit around the earth.

A rocket engine is simple. But a big multistage rocket is not at all simple. Thousands of parts may be needed to make it do what it is expected to do.

Electromagnet Lifting Scrap Iron

Pocket Compass

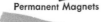

Permanent Magnets

Horseshoe
Magnet
Attracting Tacks

MAGNETS

THE BIG ROUND "cake" hanging from the derrick is a magnet. It is run by electricity. The load it is lifting is scrap iron. It will drop its load as soon as the electricity is shut off.

The horseshoe magnet is holding a load of tacks. This magnet is a magnet all the time. It will hold the tacks until someone pulls them off.

Magnets that are run by electricity are called electric magnets or electromagnets. Magnets that are magnets all the time are called permanent magnets. "Permanent" means "lasting."

The big electric magnet in the picture could not be picking up lumps of coal instead of scrap iron. The little magnet could not be picking up pennies instead of tacks. Magnets pick up loads of iron or steel only. They pull, or attract, some other materials a little, but not enough to count.

It looks like magic to see magnets picking up loads. Their "fingers" are not bothered by sharp edges or by heat. They can pick up jagged pieces of scrap iron and sharp-pointed tacks without any trouble. In steel mills big electric magnets often move red-hot chunks of steel.

Magnets are made in many, many different shapes and sizes. Some of them can pick up much bigger loads than others.

The "magic fingers" of a magnet are not always used for picking things up. Sometimes they are used for pointing. The needle of a pocket compass is a tiny magnet that can turn around easily. If nothing interferes with it, it turns until it points north. The other directions are easy to tell as soon as one knows which way is north. Compasses are a big help to sailors and explorers.

Electricity for Light

JACK-OF-ALL-TRADES

Electricity does much more for us than make big lifting magnets work. The pictures on these pages show a few of the other ways electricity helps us. There is not nearly enough room to show all the ways. Electricity is truly a Jack-of-all-trades.

People knew about electricity back in the days of the ancient Greeks. But it was a long, long, long time before they found out how to make it do anything useful. Columbus took a magnet compass with him on his travels. But he never saw an electric magnet. In his time electricity had not yet been put to work. In George Washington's time it was still only something to experiment with. In Abraham Lincoln's time people were just beginning to see how useful it could be.

People were a long time putting electricity to work, because they were a long time finding out how to get a steady flow of it. They could get tiny sparks, but these sparks were not useful. A steady flow of electricity is called an electric current. Today we get currents of electricity mostly from batteries or from generators. Batteries are made up of cells that have chemicals in them. Generators are machines. A cell may be as tiny as a thimble. A generator may be as big as a house. We can get weak currents or strong ones.

Before people could put electricity to work they also had to find out how to make a current go where they wanted it to go. They had to know what substances it would travel through and what ones it would not. They had to find ways of starting it and stopping it. Now we can buy all sorts and sizes of wire made of good conductors of electricity—substances that it will flow through easily. Some wire is wrapped with a poor conductor to keep the current from getting off the track. We can buy switches of many kinds for turning a current on or off.

It is wonderful to see electricity running electric

Electricity for Motors

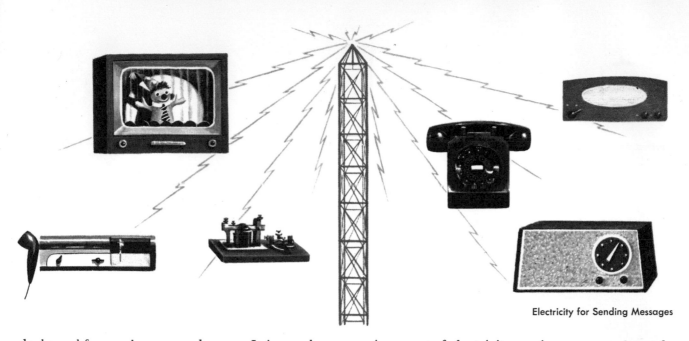

Electricity for Sending Messages

clocks and fans and vacuum cleaners. It is wonderful to see electricity turning night into day with electric lights. It is wonderful to see electricity producing heat in stoves and heaters and toasters. It seems like magic for a doctor to be able to take an X-ray picture of a broken bone right through skin and muscle. It is even more like magic to have an electric eye open a door for us. But perhaps electricity amazes us most as a messenger. It carries telegraph messages and telephone messages and cablegrams. Radio would be impossible without it. So would television.

Some people think that when they talk over a telephone the sound of their voices travels along the telephone wires. It doesn't. Only a current of electricity travels along the wires. Talking into a telephone sends this messenger on its way. When it gets to the end of the line it makes the telephone receiver repeat the message.

A current of electricity carries messages through telegraph wires and through cables under the sea, too. An electric current does not travel from the broadcasting stations to our radio and television sets. Instead, invisible waves bring the programs to us. But currents of electricity start these waves on their way and run the sets to receive them. They turn sights and sounds into waves and then turn the waves back into sights and sounds again.

Messages travel by wires and waves marvelously fast. Over the telephone a person in New York can talk with a person in San Francisco just as if the two were in the same room. By radio we can hear a concert from across the ocean as quickly as if we were in the back of the concert hall. By television we can see a baseball player hit a home run only a tiny part of a second later than the people at the game see him. Our Jack-of-all-trades brings the world right into our houses.

Electricity for Heat

83

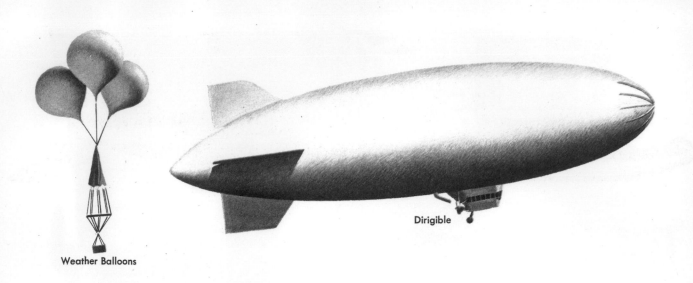

Weather Balloons

Dirigible

FLOATING

A BALL that is dropped falls to the ground. A sled at the top of a hill slides to the bottom. The earth pulls the ball and the sled down. The pull of the earth is called gravity.

Gravity is very important. If it weren't for gravity everything on the earth that was not fastened down would go sailing off into space. And nothing on the earth would weigh anything. For weight is just a measure of how hard the earth is pulling.

The earth is pulling on the balloons in the picture. But they have gone high in the air. They are floating there. Balloons of this kind go high in the air because they are filled with a gas that is lighter than the air close to the earth. The earth is pulling the balloons, but it is pulling the air close to the ground harder. The heavier air pushes the balloons up. Some gases are so much lighter than air that balloons filled with them can lift heavy loads.

Air, in turn, is very much lighter than water. Knowing this has helped men build boats that can carry heavy cargoes. The big boats of today are made partly of steel, which is much heavier than water. But a boat is hollow. It floats because the air inside weighs so little. Even with a big load of passengers and with big engines to drive it, it still is light enough to float.

Ocean Liner

Airliner

Phantom Fighter

FLYING

BIRDS FLY through the air. They do not float. Birds are lighter than other animals of the same size, but they are not light enough to float. If a bird in mid-air should fold its wings in close to its body and hold them there, it would come tumbling down.

Airplanes fly through the air, too. And they are much, much heavier than air. If an airplane should stop moving forward, it would take a nose dive at once.

Birds push themselves through the air by beating their wings against the air. As they move forward the air pushes harder on the underside of their wings than on the top. It does so because of the shape of the birds' wings. The greater push on the underside is enough to hold the birds in

the air. To keep itself in the air a bird must not only spread its wings but it must keep moving.

The engines of airplanes push them through the air. The engines may turn propellers. They may push the airplane by shooting out jets of gas. As the airplane rushes through the air, the air pushes harder on the underside of the wings than on the top. The wings of a plane are shaped so that it will. The air pushes enough harder on the underside to let the plane carry a heavy load. But if a plane stops moving, the air pushes down on the wings just as hard as it pushes up. The earth's gravity then pulls the plane down in a hurry.

Air Flow Past Wing of Plane

WONDERS OF TODAY
AND TOMORROW

EVEN IN ancient times people were wonderful builders. Seven of the things they built were so remarkable that they are called the Seven Wonders of the World. Some of the Seven Wonders were tombs or temples, and some were giant statues. The walls of a city were one of the wonders, and a lighthouse was another.

These ancient wonders were remarkable because in those days builders did not have giant machines to help them. They did not have steel and many of the other materials we have now to work with.

With our machines and materials we have built many wonders. The pictures on this page show a few. Among the many others are the artificial satellites we have made for exploring space.

Sputnik I

Vanguard I

Discoverer XIII

Telstar I

Transit's Pickaback
Satellite TRAAC

Transit IV-B

OSO I

Tiros III

Explorer XIII

Echo I

The space age began in 1957 when the Soviet Union launched the little satellite called Sputnik I. Early in 1958 the first American satellite, Explorer I, was launched. These satellites were unmanned. They did not, that is, carry any people aloft in them. Since the first satellites were launched, dozens of unmanned satellites have been carried up and put into orbit around either the earth or the sun. Those that are sent into orbit around the earth are sometimes called artificial moons. Those that are sent into orbit around the sun are sometimes called artificial asteroids.

Satellites, as you know, are carried aloft and put into orbit by multistage rockets. Some of our satellites stay in orbit much longer than others. Vanguard I, the second satellite launched by the United States, is expected to stay in orbit for a thousand years. The Soviet Union and the United States both have satellites traveling around the sun. These satellites are expected to travel around the sun forever. But some unmanned satellites stay in orbit only a few weeks or even days.

Every satellite launched has some mission to perform. Almost every one carries a radio transmitter for sending messages back to earth. It may send back pictures, too.

There have been more than forty Discoverers. They have carried many instruments aloft and sent them back by parachute. These instruments have found out a great deal about the upper air.

Tiros satellites send down pictures of the earth's cloud cover. They are weather satellites.

Transit satellites help in navigation. They let sailors find out where they are more easily than by looking at the sun and stars.

"OSO" stands for "orbiting solar observatory." OSO satellites are sent up to study the sun.

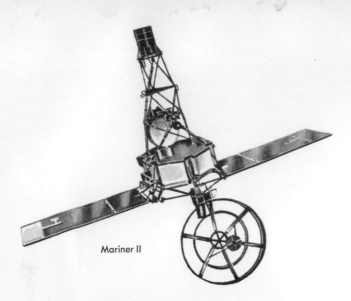
Mariner II

Echo and Telstar belong in the group of communications satellites. These satellites are put into orbit to help with sending radio and television programs to distant stations.

Explorer satellites have sent back word of meteors, of temperatures aloft, and of a belt of dangerous radiation. Explorer XIII was the fiftieth satellite launched by the United States.

Mariner II is one of the satellites the United States has sent far out beyond our ocean of air. On its way into an orbit around the sun, it sent back, late in 1962, much information about the planet Venus. Satellites like Mariner, that collect information as they pass heavenly bodies, are often called "fly-by" satellites.

Both the United States and the Soviet Union have sent up manned satellites, too. They are called space capsules. One of the big problems in building a space capsule was how to build the capsule so that it could come back to the earth's surface safely. Unmanned satellites burn up as they fall through the air at the end of their journeys.

The Americans who have become space explorers are called astronauts. The space explorers of the Soviet Union are called cosmonauts.

The one-man American space capsules are called Mercury capsules. In a Mercury space cabin the astronaut lies on a couch that is much like a big easy chair. In front and to the side of him he has instruments with which he can control the flight of his spacecraft. The Gemini capsule is planned to carry two astronauts around the earth perhaps for as long as a week.

An astronaut wears a special space suit. The suit is pressurized to keep the spaceman's blood from boiling. At great heights above the ground the air pressure is so low that no one could survive without some way of increasing pressure. The helmet of the suit contains an oxygen mask which allows the spaceman to get the oxygen he needs from a tank of oxygen. The suit includes heavy gloves, for even his hands must be protected from the dangers of airlessness.

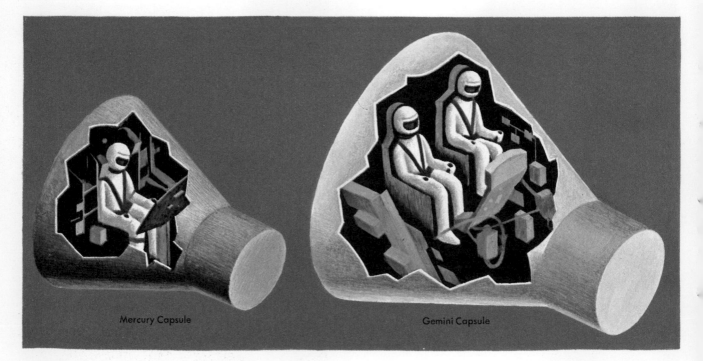
Mercury Capsule   Gemini Capsule

Rocket Ship Approaching Space Station

Of course, explorers are interested in going beyond our ocean of air. One of the first trips away from the earth will certainly be a trip to the moon. Several unmanned satellites have reached the moon. Giant rockets are already being built that will be powerful enough to send a spaceship with passengers to the moon. Later there will be trips to Mars and other planets. Spaceships that can carry explorers on such long journeys are among the wonders to come.

Perhaps another of the wonders of tomorrow will be a space station circling the earth far, far above its surface. It would not take nearly so powerful a rocket to launch a spaceship from such a station as it would take to launch one from the earth. And returning spaceships could land at such a station without any danger of burning up from rushing through the air.

A number of plans have been made for a space station. The picture at the top of the page shows one scientist's idea of what a space station might be like. The rim of the big wheel would be hollow and would be broken up into living quarters, laboratories, and workrooms. The hub of the wheel could be the landing field and take-off area for moon-bound or planet-bound spaceships.

A space station would have to be big—far too big to be built on the ground and then carried up by a rocket and put into its orbit. The station would have to start with a small satellite put into an orbit about a thousand miles up. Then rockets would have to carry up men and materials so that the little satellite could be built into a big space station. Perhaps the men at work on the space station would wear suits much like those astronauts now wear. Perhaps "bottle-suits" would be better —suits so loose that a workman could move around a bit inside them.

Beams of light sent out by a device called a laser and carrying 100,000 phone calls at once may be another wonder to come. And no doubt there are wonders ahead no one yet dreams of.

Nonluminous, or Light-reflecting

Luminous, or Light-giving

Mirror

Lenses

Prism

LIGHT

WITHOUT LIGHT we could not see anything at all. Light must come to our eyes from the star or cloud or dog or anything else we see. The light may be given off by the thing itself. We see stars and lighted candles and flashing fireflies because they give off light of their own. Things that give off light of their own are called luminous. We see mice and flowers and magazines because some of the light that reaches them from the sun or lamps or flaming fires bounces into our eyes. The light, we say, is reflected. Things that we see with the light from something else are called nonluminous.

Light travels so fast that in a single second it can travel as far as $7\frac{1}{2}$ times around the earth at the equator. But no beam of light ever curved round and round the earth. Light travels in straight lines. Many times we hear someone around a corner talking when we cannot see him. Light does not bend around corners as sound does.

In every thunderstorm we are reminded that light travels very fast. For we see a flash of lightning before we hear the thunder caused by the flash. The light from the lightning reaches us in almost no time at all. It may take several seconds for the sound to reach us.

Mirrors, lenses, and prisms are big helps in seeing. Mirrors reflect light so well that we can see ourselves in them. Lenses bend the light that passes through them so that they make things look larger or smaller, nearer or farther away. Prisms can be used as mirrors. With them we can also break up sunlight into the seven rainbow colors it is made up of: violet, indigo, blue, green, yellow, orange, and red.

SHADOWS

LIGHT can shine through some substances so well that we can see through them. We say that these substances are transparent. Window glass is transparent. So are air and water and cellophane.

Some substances let some light through but not enough to let us see through them. Waxed paper is a good example. Some substances do not let any light through. Walls of brick or stone or wood, for instance, shut out all light.

When sunlight is shining on a tree, it cannot shine through the leaves and trunk and branches. The tree casts a shadow. Anything that is not transparent will cast a shadow if light is shining on it from just one direction.

Every one of us casts a shadow if we are in the sunshine. No one can get away from his shadow except by going into the shadow of something else. But a person's shadow does not always look the same. When the sun is high in the sky our shadows are shorter than we are. When the sun is low in the sky they are longer than we are tall.

The earth casts a shadow. Its shadow is the shape of an ice-cream cone. As the moon travels around the earth, it sometimes gets into the earth's shadow. We say that there is an eclipse of the moon.

The moon casts a shadow, too. Its shadow is also cone-shaped. Sometimes, as the moon travels around the earth, its shadow hits the earth. For the people in the shadow of the moon there is an eclipse of the sun.

Long ago people used shadows to tell time. They built sundials. We have better ways of telling time now. But just for fun some people still have sundials in their gardens.

Shadow at Mid-day

Shadow in Mid-afternoon

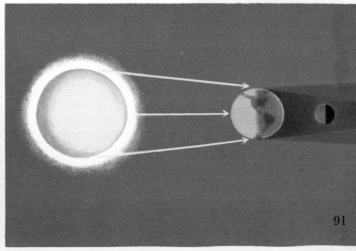

Shadow at Sunset

Eclipse of Sun

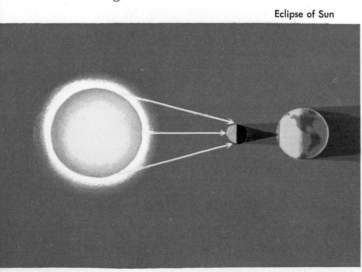

Eclipse of Moon

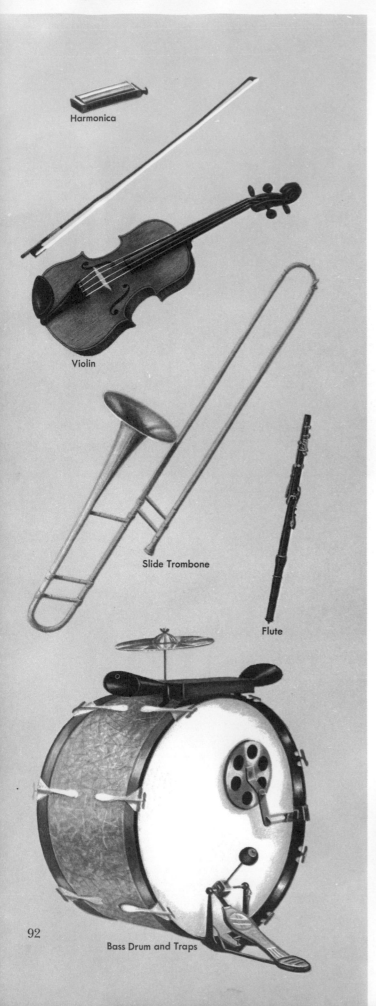

Harmonica

Violin

Slide Trombone

Flute

Bass Drum and Traps

SOUND

RUSTLE, rumble, roar; scream, shriek, screech; whisper, warble, whimper; murmur, slam, purr. These are only a few of the names we have for different sounds. We need many such names, because there are ever and ever so many different sounds.

Some sounds are soft. Some are loud. Some sounds are high. Some are low. Some sounds are pleasant. Some are unpleasant. But they are all made in the same way. They are all made by the rapid vibrating of something. "Vibrating" means "moving back and forth."

When leaves rustle, the wind is making them move back and forth. When a lion roars, the vocal cords in the lion's throat are vibrating. When a door slams, the wood of the door and the door frame is vibrating.

Some sounds are so pleasant that we call them music. In some musical instruments strings vibrate to make the sound. In others the air inside vibrates. In still others a sheet of metal or skin vibrates.

Sound is usually carried to our ears through the air. The sound waves that travel to us through the air are a little like ripples in water. But of course we cannot see them.

Sound can travel through other materials. It travels through some of them faster than through air. The picture of the hunter shows how the early settlers of our country tried to find out whether any Indians were approaching. Sound travels very well through solid ground. We can understand how the saying "putting one's ear to the ground" came about.

ECHOES

WHEN sound waves strike a solid wall they bounce back. The boy in the picture hears twice every note he blows on his bugle. He hears it once as he makes it. He hears it again after the sound waves have had time to travel across the lake and back. The rock wall at the other side of the lake sends them back. When sound waves are bent back in this way, we say that there is an echo.

If the lake in the picture is half a mile across, the boy hears the echo of a note just five seconds after he blows it. For it takes sound five seconds to travel a mile.

The boy might shout some words across the lake instead of blowing his bugle. Words as well as notes can come back as echoes.

Some places are famous for their echoes. In Ireland there are some small lakes with mountains all around them. A bugle note sounded on the shore of one of these little lakes may be echoed a hundred times.

But a person does not have to go to a mountain lake to hear echoes. Any blank wall makes a good mirror for sound. A blank wall is one without any windows in it. A person should not stand too close to a wall if he wants to hear his echo. He should be at least 50 feet away. If he stands closer, the echo will get back to him so soon that his shout and the echo seem to be all one.

Echoes can be a nuisance. In concert halls curtains often have to be hung on the walls to prevent echoes. Echoes are fun to experiment with, but they can spoil a concert.

TOYS THAT WORK

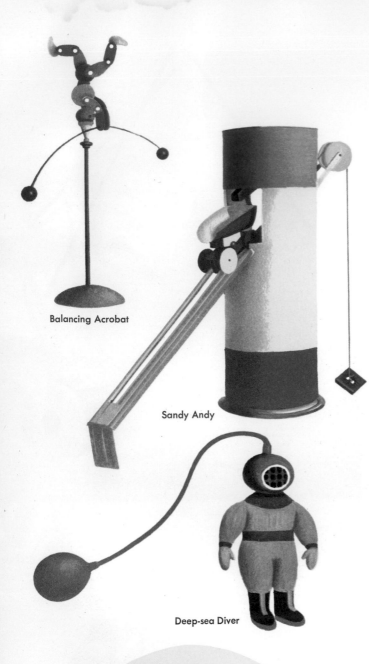

Balancing Acrobat

Sandy Andy

Deep-sea Diver

Dart Game

Jack-in-the-Box

THE LITTLE toy acrobat can balance at the top of his pole in all sorts of positions. The metal balls hold him in place. They are much heavier than he is. Gravity holds them down, and they hold the little man in place.

A Sandy Andy is a gravity toy, too. The hopper at the top is filled with sand. The little car is pulled up the slope by a weight. When it reaches the top, the hopper opens. The car fills with sand. As soon as it is full of sand, it is heavier than the weight. It then rolls downhill. The sand empties out, and up the car comes again.

The deep-sea diver is hollow. When he is put in water, he fills up with water. Then he sinks. As soon as the bulb is squeezed and air is forced in to push out the water, the diver comes up to the top. He comes to the top because, with air inside him, he is light enough to float.

Each of the darts for the dart game has a little rubber cup at the end. It has air in it. When the dart hits the target, the air in the cup is squeezed out. Then the air on the outside pushes against the cup and holds the dart on the target. The dart stays on the target until air leaks in.

The jack-in-the-box works with a spring. When the lid of the box is closed, the coils of the spring inside the clown are pushed close together. When the lid is opened, the coils spring apart and up pops the clown.

Each of the fishing rods for the fish pond game has a tiny horseshoe magnet at the end. The fish have iron rings in their heads. The magnets attract the iron rings.

A kaleidoscope has mirrors in it. It also has bits of colored glass or plastic in it. The reflections of the colored bits in the mirrors make pretty patterns. Turning the kaleidoscope makes the patterns change. One looks into a kaleidoscope through a rather small hole.

The music of the toy music box is made by a tiny comb of metal. A small metal barrel with little bumps on it in just the right spots turns round and round, and the bumps strike one tooth of the comb after another and set them to vibrating. Each tooth makes a different note. In this way the music box can play tunes. The little metal barrel is turned by a spring.

An electric train is a complicated toy. Some trains are more complicated than others. Electricity comes to the engine through one rail. It makes a motor inside the engine run. The motor turns the wheels and drives the train along the track. In the train in the picture little electric magnets hold the cars together. There are tiny electric lights on the engine and in the caboose. A tiny electric heater in the smokestack makes the engine smoke when a smoke pellet is dropped into the smokestack. In the train electricity is also used to produce sound. The tender has an electric whistle in it.

Some people may be surprised to find pictures of toys in a science book. But a person has to know a great deal of science to understand how all these toys work.

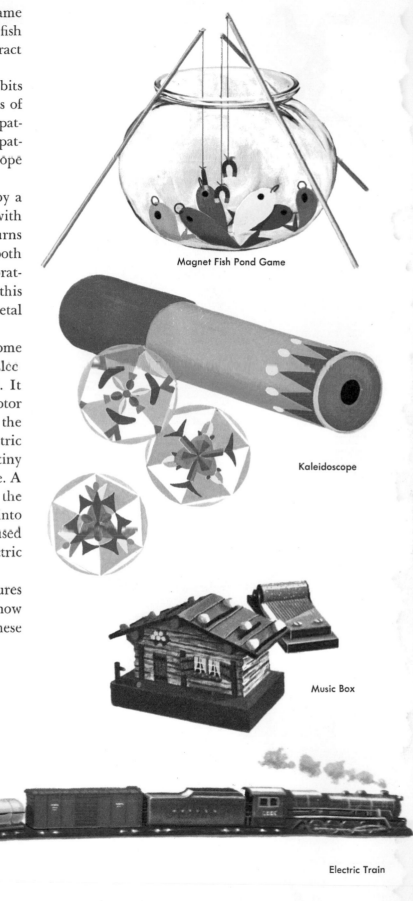

Magnet Fish Pond Game

Kaleidoscope

Music Box

Electric Train

BUILDING BLOCKS

THERE ARE hundreds of thousands of kinds of substances in the world. Queer as it seems, they are all made out of about a hundred simple substances. Scientists call these simple substances elements. They are the building blocks out of which everything else is made.

Some elements are rare. Some are common. The list below names 30 of the well-known ones.

Element	Symbol	Element	Symbol
Aluminum	Al	Neon	Ne
Argon	A	Nickel	Ni
Calcium	Ca	Nitrogen	N
Carbon	C	Oxygen	O
Chlorine	Cl	Phosphorus	P
Chromium	Cr	Platinum	Pt
Copper	Cu	Potassium	K
Gold	Au	Silicon	Si
Helium	H	Silver	Ag
Hydrogen	H	Sodium	Na
Iodine	I	Sulphur	S
Iron	Fe	Tin	Sn
Lead	Pb	Tungsten	W
Magnesium	Mg	Uranium	U
Mercury	Hg	Zinc	Zn

The symbols are the scientists' shorthand way of writing the names of the elements. It is easy to see why O stands for oxygen. But why does Au stand for gold? The reason is that gold has been known for a very long time. The ancient Romans called it *aurum*. The Au comes, then, from an old name for gold. The other queer symbols in the list came about in very much the same way.

Many elements are gases. Many are solid substances. A few are liquids.

The tiniest particle of any element is an atom. The tiniest particle of uranium, for instance, is an atom of uranium. Most kinds of atoms are too small to be seen with even the most powerful microscopes. A speck of uranium the size of a period has in it more than a billion times as many atoms as there are people on the earth.

Many substances are compounds. They are made of different kinds of atoms joined together. The smallest particle of a compound is a molecule.

It is not at all easy to tell what elements are in a compound. Sodium is a silvery metal. Chlorine is a greenish gas. But common salt is made of sodium and chlorine and nothing else. Water is made up of two gases—hydrogen and oxygen. Sugar is a compound of hydrogen, oxygen, and carbon. Carbon is usually a black solid.

Compounds that are very different may look alike. Alcohol and carbon tetrachloride look like water. But they are not at all the same.

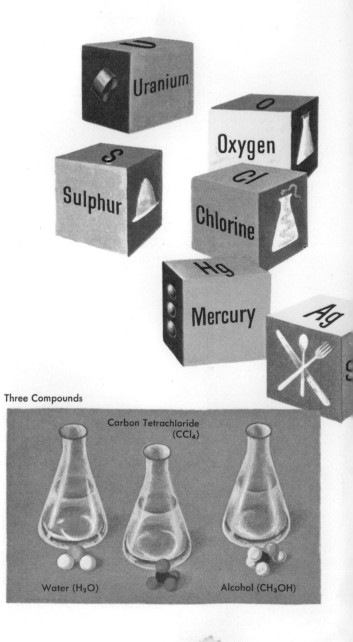

Three Compounds

Carbon Tetrachloride (CCl_4)

Water (H_2O)

Alcohol (CH_3OH)

Submarine "Nautilus"

Scientists use the symbols for the elements to tell what compounds are made of. Instead of writing "salt," for instance, they write NaCl. H_2O is water. The 2 means that there are two atoms of hydrogen to every atom of oxygen.

Scientists sometimes make little models of molecules. They use small balls to stand for atoms. In the picture of the three compounds, the black balls stand for carbon atoms, the yellow for hydrogen atoms, the blue for oxygen atoms, and the red for chlorine atoms. Of course, the little models are not supposed to really look like the molecules of these substances. No one has ever seen a molecule of any of them. Molecules, even though they may be made up of many atoms, are still almost too small for us to imagine.

Every atom of every element has a part called a nucleus. Around the nucleus one or more tiny electrons go whirling. Hydrogen atoms are the simplest. A hydrogen atom has only one electron.

Not very long ago scientists found that they could split up certain kinds of atoms. They found that they could produce a great deal of energy by doing so. The first use of atom splitting was in bombs. Now scientists are finding many better uses for it. The "Nautilus" is one of many submarines driven by atomic energy. And a number of atomic power plants have been built. So far the element most used in atom splitting is uranium.

Atomic power is sure to make life much easier for people in many parts of the world. It will be especially helpful where coal and oil are scarce. By putting the atom to work, scientists may make many wastelands into good places to live.

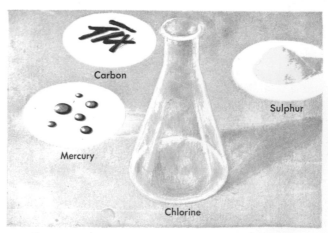

Four Elements

FIRE

FIRE was a wonderful blessing to the cave men. A burning stick was a good weapon for driving away cave bears. Fire lighted up the caves and helped keep them warm. It made it possible to cook food.

Fire has been a blessing ever since. We do not need fire to chase away cave bears. But it helps us in the other ways it helped the cave men. Besides, it runs engines and plays a part in the making of a great many things we use. Brick, steel, glass, rubber, plastics, and paper are a few of the materials made with the help of fire.

No one knows who first found out how to start a fire. If we knew who he was, he would be famous. For the invention of fire-making was one of the most important of all inventions.

Probably the earliest way of starting a fire was to rub two dry sticks together. The rubbing made the sticks hot enough to start to burn. We still use rubbing to start many fires. Striking a match means rubbing the head of a match on a rough surface. Another early way of starting a fire was to get a spark by striking two hard stones together. In cigarette lighters we still start fires with sparks.

We must not think of fire as always a friend. It can do great harm. Fire has burned down great forests. It has burned down whole cities. It has killed many people.

One good way of fighting a fire is to smother it. Fire needs air in order to burn. Shutting off air will put it out. Some chemicals are good for smothering fire. Cooling whatever is burning is another good way of fighting fire. Water is a great help in fighting most fires because it cools off the material that is burning.

"Fire is a good servant but a bad master." This is an old saying, but it is still very true.

DISCOVERIES

THE NORTH POLE has been discovered. So has the South Pole. The highest mountain on earth, Mount Everest, has been climbed. Explorers have even gone to the bottom of the ocean's deepest deep.

But boys and girls will not have to go on a journey into space to be explorers. They can make discoveries in science. Scientists are the chief explorers of today. They are making discoveries about the world around them by working right in their own laboratories.

The first scientists had very few tools to work with. Now they have a great many. They have microscopes for seeing things too small to be seen with their eyes alone. They have telescopes for seeing things too far away to be seen without help. They have scales that can weigh a single grain of sand. The pictures on page 75 show some of the instruments the weathermen use. Every science has its own tools. A science catalogue may be hundreds of pages thick.

No one should plan to be a scientist unless he is willing to work hard. He must be patient, too. He may have to work a long time to make a discovery. But he is sure to get a big thrill when he makes one.

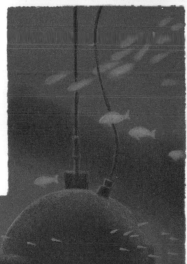

INDEX

The letters IFC refer to the Inside Front Cover,
and IBC to the Inside Back Cover

101

Weather Phenomena

Chemical Laboratory

Northern Lights